STARTUP
SCALEUP
SCREWUP

STARTUP SCALEUP SCREWUP

42 Tools to Accelerate Lean & Agile Business Growth

Jurgen Appelo

WILEY

Cover design: Juan M. Franco

Published by John Wiley & Sons, Inc., Hoboken, New Jersey.
Published simultaneously in Canada.

For general information on our other products and services or for technical support, please contact our Customer Care Department within the United States at (800) 762-2974, outside the United States at (317) 572-3993 or fax (317) 572-4002.

Wiley publishes in a variety of print and electronic formats and by print-on-demand. Some material included with standard print versions of this book may not be included in e-books or in print-on-demand. If this book refers to media such as a CD or DVD that is not included in the version you purchased, you may download this material at http://booksupport.wiley.com. For more information about Wiley products, visit www.wiley.com.

ISBN 9781119526858 (Hardcover)
ISBN 9781119526889 (ePDF)
ISBN 9781119526797 (ePub)

Printed in the United States of America

V10008653_030819

This book is dedicated to Amnon.
It is a joy and privilege to be your friend. Next to you, I look almost normal.

Contents

Prologue

I have a cunning plan.

My plan involves unifying the methods and tools that are successfully used by startups and scaleups with the principles and practices popularized by Lean and Agile communities. It includes upgrading the global Management 3.0 brand that I launched 10 years ago from just leadership practices to all areas of running a business. My plan is also about revolutionizing the way that people learn how to improve themselves and transform their organizations. At many points during the execution of this plan, I foresee travels, discussions, coffees, and lengthy rants on my social media accounts.

Then I hear the signal of our washing machine and I snap back to reality.

I was daydreaming again. What on Earth was I thinking? I cannot even get my startup team to stick to a plan. How am I going to get the rest of the world to pay attention to what I think is important? I'm not a coach or consultant. Helping other businesses to transform the way they work is not my job, nor my field of expertise. I'm just sharing my experiences while running my startups. I would be a terrible adviser. As I always say, I find my own problems much more interesting than those of other companies. And I have many!

It makes me feel like an imposter sometimes. The only thing I'm an expert at is learning tons of things that might help me solve my problems, and then sharing my insights publicly along the way. Fortunately, people seem to appreciate that. So I suppose there's no need to feel too embarrassed when I get things wrong occasionally. As long as I shout it loud and clear, "I learned something new!" The audience is welcome to learn along with me.

It's a Sunday today. It's the best day for some reflection, except when the washing machine keeps beeping. What a horrible thing.

This book is nearly finished. I'm glad I decided to write it. I learned so much this past year from all the research that I performed and all the interviews that I did all over Europe. I'm convinced that my business is better off now because of the many things I picked up that we could implement right away. I might even suggest that all startup founders write their own books. I would read them for sure.

It's quite a busy Sunday, actually. Apart from finishing and reflecting on the book, I have more work to do for the launch of our team's next crowdfunding round, which, quite miraculously, starts the day after I have sent the manuscript of this book to the publisher. It also seems that quite a few people are waiting to hear about my new Shiftup workshop program, for which I will use the ideas that I had while writing this book. Maybe I can do some thinking on that tonight, after a bike ride in the forest.

Oh, forget it. There is no cunning plan.

I'm just winging it, like most other founders, entrepreneurs, intrapreneurs, and business leaders. I try a thousand things, and a dozen of them seem to work. That's how I'm more successful than some other people because they often try nothing. If there's one thing that I learned over the past 20 years, it's to fail often and fail small. That's how founders and leaders do many things, of which a few will be a great success. This book is just one of many things.

Now for heaven's sake, which product designer thought it was a great idea to let a washing machine keep beeping?

Persistence of Vision

Inspire team members, customers, and investors with a Product Vision: a mental image of your desired future.

Many of us are visionaries. As entrepreneurs, intrapreneurs, founders, leaders, and creatives, we envision things that do not yet exist. We want those things to become real.

For example:

Wouldn't it be great if there were no bad jobs, no bad managers, and no bad companies? Wouldn't it be awesome if everything we knew about doing better work was somehow stored in data and algorithms in such a way that machines helped us to improve our organizations? Wouldn't it be great if, someday in the not-so-far future, rather than us telling computers how to do mindless work, they helped us do *meaningful* work?

Someday, machines will understand how teams of people do their best work together. They will offer us suggestions, such as, "You might want to clean up your product backlog after yesterday's customer demo"; and "This was your 500th daily cafe. How about celebrating it? I have an idea for you to surprise your team"; and "Hey, your last agile retrospective was six weeks ago. Here is a new retro exercise that's popular right now in your industry."

Who needs managers watching over people's shoulders when artificial intelligence will be able to help teams to hire people, guide performance, and achieve organizational change? A smart business is the kind of company I want my startup to be! Everyone loving their jobs. Everyone trying to make things better. And intelligent machines helping us to improve our work. As far as I know, machine learning algorithms have no interest in the top floor corner office, a limousine with driver, or the parking space next to the office entrance. We would save tons of money on management perks, bonuses, and printed PowerPoint slide decks!

What I just described is only a vision. But it's a nice one. I believe that innovation often starts with visionaries.

As an entrepreneur, intrapreneur, founder, leader, or creative, you need a Product Vision. It describes the essence of an innovative product: what it aims to achieve for its users and customers. A great Product Vision helps people to mentally visualize what value should be delivered, as if they're hearing a short story about a successful business in the future.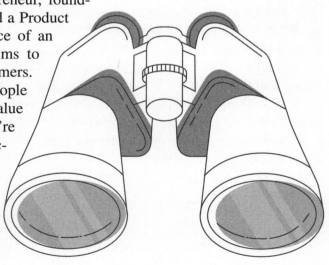

Michał Borkowski, founder and CEO of Brainly, had a few minutes to spare for me at Brainly's office in Kraków, Poland. The company was

growing so fast, they literally occupied a temporary office in between their old and new offices.

> *We defined the opportunity ahead of us in a way that scales globally. There are 1.2 billion students in the world and every student needs help learning every day. If we think about the problem that Brainly is solving, it's that big problem. Quite often, what I see is that the problems that startups are trying to solve are not big enough. They are chasing an opportunity that is way smaller than the real opportunity that is ahead of them. It was the same for us early on. We started in Poland. We were initially not thinking about our global opportunity. We were just thinking about our own country. It took us about three years to really figure out why we are here and what we are trying to achieve. Now that it's clearly defined, it helps me to manage the company towards that vision. I would encourage every startup founder and CEO to think about their big vision way earlier than we have done.*
> *Michał Borkowski, founder and CEO of Brainly, Kraków, Poland*

The reason that we craft a vision is to have a direction in which to navigate with our team's product development efforts. We can dream our dreams and then formulate a vision without knowing anything about available technologies, markets, or revenue streams. We figure out the details later. The first thing we need to do is to inspire ourselves and our cofounders, if we have them, our first team members, if we want them, and any investors, if we need them. Without the inspiration of the people around us, nobody will care about figuring out the details of how to get there. Without a vision, there probably won't be a realization of the dream.

Don't confuse a Product Vision with a strategic plan. Sharing a dream with your team is not about a list of features on a Product Roadmap. A vision is not a carefully crafted statement concocted by a committee on a two-day retreat in a wellness resort. A vision is not the slogan on a mug filled with a cappuccino that was excreted from a push-button machine. Instead, your vision is a verbal image of the future, in language that you would use when you told your story in a bar, to convince your friends to help you make things happen. And the vision is big, bold, and compelling. *I have a dream* comes before *I have a team*. It is what separates the great leaders from the failed ones.

Marc Wesselink, managing partner at Startupbootcamp, spoke enthusiastically across the large table of the shared meeting room in Amsterdam. The building was full of startups and, what seemed to me, a well-organized creative chaos.

> *When I look at all the dozens or hundreds of startups that went by, the great ones have something that the others don't. There is one thing that makes all the difference. The best founders have a True North. They have some sort of clock ticking in them that they want to solve a huge problem. But then, in what way and how and to which customers, that's not certain yet. They are willing to be flexible, as long as they can make progress toward their vision. That's, by far, the biggest differentiator.*
> *Marc Wesselink, managing partner at Startupbootcamp,*
> *Amsterdam, The Netherlands*

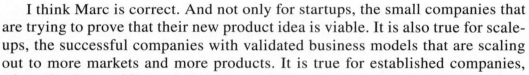

I think Marc is correct. And not only for startups, the small companies that are trying to prove that their new product idea is viable. It is also true for scaleups, the successful companies with validated business models that are scaling out to more markets and more products. It is true for established companies, whose leaders and intrapreneurs are trying to transform and reinvent their organizations so that they are not outmaneuvered and replaced by the startups and the scaleups.

An often-heard complaint about management in mature organizations is the lack of a clear direction. Employees are all busy selling products and services, but nobody knows where the company is heading. None of the workers feel inspired by a dream for a better future. To address this concern, the business leaders of traditional companies need to communicate a shared vision. And they need to do so consistently and persistently. It makes a huge difference to the creativity, collaboration, and commitment of teams when they are shown a big, bold dream. This enables them to envision the future results of their work. Nobody dreams about ordinary product features, unless they are nightmares. But imagining how the world is going to change in the future, and how the work that they're doing is contributing to that future, *that* is worth dreaming about. People need to say, "If *that's* going to be possible soon, count me in. I want to make it happen!"

I tried not to make a mess of my wet tea bag on a large, black table somewhere in Helsinki, Finland, while Jenni Tolonen explained to me the original vision of the company Management Events, of which she is now the CEO.

> *Our founder wanted us to help Finnish people be more social at business-to-business events and bring them together. In today's very digital world, if the face-to-face contacts are well-facilitated and they are matched around common interests, and the environment is fun and engaging, people can generate good business. They can make new contacts. They can get new ideas. Maybe they even get their problems solved. That's what our founder wanted, so that's where our vision lies. And we're happy that we have made good progress toward that vision.*
> *Jenni Tolonen, CEO at Management Events, Helsinki, Finland*

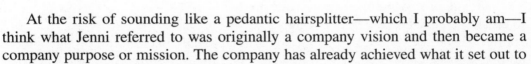

At the risk of sounding like a pedantic hairsplitter—which I probably am—I think what Jenni referred to was originally a company vision and then became a company purpose or mission. The company has already achieved what it set out to do. They have realized their dream and now they want to do more of it. Following commonly accepted definitions, a company's purpose (sometimes referred to as its mission) is about the present. It explains why it does the things it does. A vision is about the future. It explains the lofty goal the organization hopes to achieve. Having a purpose is about being meaningful; having a vision is about being hopeful. Mission is push. Vision is pull. And that's as far as I will go with the pedantic hairsplitting.

An inspiring example of a vision is The Ocean Cleanup, a nonprofit organization headquartered in my hometown, Rotterdam, The Netherlands. With passive drifting systems and advanced technologies, and by using the natural currents of the oceans, this organization wants to clean up half the Great Pacific Garbage Patch in just five years' time. At the time of writing, the company claims to be ahead of schedule. The 24-year-old Boyan Slat, founder and CEO of The Ocean Cleanup, considered his vision so important that he turned it into the company's name!

One of the many reasons why companies fail and screw up is a lack of passion or commitment of the leaders to solve a certain problem. The business drifts to the left, and then it drifts to the right; maybe it even goes in circles. The company is like a garbage patch waiting to be cleaned up by a passionate young founder. Don't let that happen to you. Start visioning!

What is your dream? What do you care about deeply? Which vision do you want to make real? It doesn't have to be something that grabs headlines all over the world, such as cleaning up the oceans. Other problems are more important, perhaps for a smaller number of people. Your Product Vision should be simple enough for people to visualize, understand, and repeat to each other in your absence. No jargon. No buzzword bingo. No long, complicated sentences. Just a vivid, mental picture of something that could become true in the future, communicated with clarity and persistence.

I dream of computers helping us to create better work and better organizations. It is my vision of a better world. Happier workers through better technologies. Product Visions fit well in what I call the *Initiation* stage of the Shiftup Business Lifecycle. I will tell you more about that soon. All in good time. There is a lot of ground to cover in this book. Let's start with a founder story.

For related notes, articles, books, examples, and downloads, check out this web page: https://startup-scaleup-screwup.com/product-vision.

Stories of Your Life and Others

Discover the Business Lifecycle of startups and scaleups and reflect on exploration, execution, and Product/Market Fit.

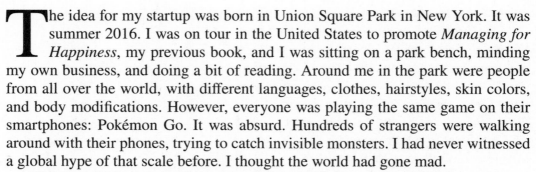

The idea for my startup was born in Union Square Park in New York. It was summer 2016. I was on tour in the United States to promote *Managing for Happiness*, my previous book, and I was sitting on a park bench, minding my own business, and doing a bit of reading. Around me in the park were people from all over the world, with different languages, clothes, hairstyles, skin colors, and body modifications. However, everyone was playing the same game on their smartphones: Pokémon Go. It was absurd. Hundreds of strangers were walking around with their phones, trying to catch invisible monsters. I had never witnessed a global hype of that scale before. I thought the world had gone mad.

Then something clicked in my head. I thought, "As business coaches, consultants, and trainers, we do our best to get people in organizations to change their behaviors. It can take years for just a few hundred employees to fully adopt agile and lean practices because organizational change is hard. And yet, within just a few weeks, millions of people are playing Pokémon Go. Isn't that behavioral change, too? How did the game's creators manage to achieve that so quickly? It's unfair!"

I realized that organizational change is often hindered because it's usually not enjoyable. There are no smart algorithms offering employees quests, treasures, levels, and badges. There are no colorful monsters to catch in the company office—and the intern that you tricked into wearing formal suit-and-tie doesn't count. Right there, I saw the opportunity that would later find its way onto the *Problem* slide of my Pitch Deck: organizational change through gamification and machine learning. That's what I wanted to try. It was the moment my startup emerged in the first stage of what I call the Shiftup Business Lifecycle.

I believe that we can visualize the typical lifecycle of startups and scaleups as a number of stages or game levels. Like in a PlayStation game, the first level is where new business ideas appear before they begin their journey up to the higher levels. The top level is where a successful business model goes to rest after wrapping up a long and prosperous life. At the other levels in between, the business model starts up, scales up, and hopefully doesn't screw things up along the way. What I find interesting is that the best rules and strategies for survival change, depending on a business model's current stage in this lifecycle. The challenges for older businesses are different from those the younger ones are facing. Moreover, the dos and don'ts for startups change significantly once they turn into scaleups. The game of business evolves with the journey.

The lifecycle of business models seems similar to the typical lifecycle of human beings. The game of life starts for us when we're newborns and, much later, when we're old, gray, and (in some cases) ready to say farewell to the world, it's game over. At the other stages in between, we are young; we grow up; and, hopefully, we survive all the monsters that life throws at us, while we keep ourselves busy completing quests, collecting treasures, and earning badges. While growing up, we learn that the things we are allowed to do when we are toddlers, like playing naked in a park, are not quite acceptable anymore when we get older. (It would have been nice if someone had warned me.) Likewise, the naughty things that we were told to stay away from as children suddenly become permissible when we're teenagers and young adults. (Again, it would have been nice if someone had briefed me earlier.) The dos and don'ts for humans depend on the stage in their lives and their level in the game. It's almost as if humans are like businesses.

Note that I refer to the lifecycle of *businesses* (which is my shorthand for *business models*), not *companies*. A startup is a temporary organization in search of a scalable, repeatable, and profitable business model. When the business model is validated, the startup turns into a scaleup. When it cannot be validated, or fails in any other way, it turns into a screwup. Failure is inevitable, because, when the business gets very old, it will screw up anyway. We're born, we grow up, we die. Simple as that.

As long as your company operates only one business model, you are dealing with just one lifecycle. But when you have an established company that launches new business models, it is like a family having kids. The offspring has its own lifecycle. The parent business model funds the young ones, and while the parent gets older, the kids start their journeys from the beginning. Young business lifecycles cannot exist without supportive ecosystems in which to be alive.

As a leader, you may be dealing with multiple business models in various lifecycle stages. Your company is just a legal and financial container. When you organize things well, what will start up, scale up, and occasionally screw up, are your business models, not the company itself. Your company is a family. By always renewing itself, it can exist for a very long time. Indeed, many families in this world go back centuries.

I've noticed many times that leaders and entrepreneurs usually screw things up when they do the wrong things in the wrong stage of the Business Lifecycle. For example, startup founders often try to scale up their business without having validated most aspects of their business model. That's as dangerous as a kid driving a car without having earned his driver's license. Other entrepreneurs simply have not prepared for the next stage and then experience significant problems when the environment shoves them into it. That's as naive as a young adult finishing her studies and then still not knowing how to earn her living. At the other end of the scale, it is common for leaders of established businesses to treat new business ideas as formal projects that are expected to forecast their sales, budgets, return on investment (ROI), and net present value (NPV). That's like requiring children to calculate how they're going to pay you back for their cost of living.

I believe that a lack of awareness of Business Lifecycle stages, and their context-dependent rules and practices, is the main reason for screw ups in business. Being aware of where your business is on the typical path will help you anticipate the challenges that you will be facing soon. It will also help you manage your business model correctly according to the natural stage in its life cycle. For the best chance at shifting up to the highest level, kids and grownups need different freedoms and constraints at different levels in the game.

Let's have a look at the 10 levels of the Shiftup Business Lifecycle (Figure 2.1).

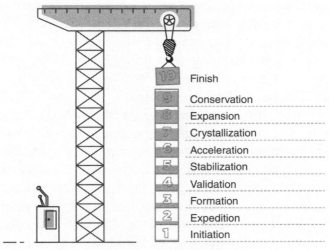

FIGURE 2.1   The Shiftup Business Lifecycle

In the **Initiation stage (1)**, your business is just an idea for a new product or service. It has no agency of its own yet. Like a newborn, it needs regular care and attention or else it just withers and dies.

You might call it the familiarization or the preparation level. It is the level at which you start exploring the feasibility and viability of the idea and your purpose as a founder/entrepreneur or an intrapreneur of a corporate startup. In this stage, you earn your income with another role or job, and perhaps you have some discussions with friends or colleagues who, at the next levels, might become your cofounders or team members.

What you need to complete at this first level is your Product Vision and any preparations for seeking Product/Solution Fit, which is the search that happens at the next level. This stage ends when you have been able to secure a small amount of time and resources to start the research and begin the actual game.

The **Expedition stage (2)** is the infant level of your startup. In this stage, everything is done to check the vitality of the idea and to keep the infant alive. At this level, you become a business founder or startup leader because you found a way to pay for further exploration and development of your idea, through bootstrapping or with some pre-seed money from the three Fs: your friends, your family, or your formal or former employer.

The focus of this stage, sometimes referred to as Customer Discovery, is on forming the initial team of cofounders, developing a strategy, and defining the first business model hypotheses that will need to be validated. Most importantly, you must figure out if the product you have in mind is indeed something that customers want to have, by talking with many people and testing your most important hypotheses. Part of this can be done with a low-fidelity Minimum Viable Product, which is the simplest possible prototype of your product that enables you to measure the responses of potential clients.

The stage ends when you have confirmed that you have Problem/Solution Fit. You found a problem that is worth solving; a specific group of target users is willing to pay for your proposed solution (viability), which you are also able to build (feasibility).

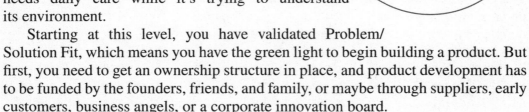

It's only in the **Formation stage (3)** that you become a true founder or business leader. Your startup is a toddler now. It starts communicating and behaving with a mind of its own, but it still needs daily care while it's trying to understand its environment.

Starting at this level, you have validated Problem/ Solution Fit, which means you have the green light to begin building a product. But first, you need to get an ownership structure in place, and product development has to be funded by the founders, friends, and family, or maybe through suppliers, early customers, business angels, or a corporate innovation board.

In this stage, you and your cofounders are in the process of becoming fully committed to the new business. After all, when founders cannot even convince themselves to quit their regular jobs and invest some of their own resources in the company, the idea is probably not big enough for others to care about.

This stage may involve shareholder agreements, option agreements, compensation agreements, and professional advisors. At the end of this level, you have achieved Vision/Founders Fit: The cofounders agree that they're in it for the long term to realize their vision. Up to this third stage, the toddler could get away with just playing and tinkering. However, after this level, growing up gets more serious!

In the **Validation stage (4)**, the young child starts learning, either by going to school or by not burning the house down. Your startup begins its work on seeking Product/Market Fit: validating all business model hypotheses. This stage is the most difficult for many startups. At this level, you keep proving the assumptions of your business model until you can show the first signs of traction, growth, and revenue. You learn everything you can about your customers while trying to burn your cash as slowly as possible. You spend most of your time tweaking, patching, and sometimes pivoting, creating high-fidelity Minimum Viable Products that steadily evolve from early prototypes into near-finished product releases.

In the Validation stage, you validate not only the success of the product but also the size of the market. You have completed this stage when the product is well received, and the market turns out to be large. However, because this level is by definition a search in unknown territory, it might take several additional rounds of funding to get there. At the end of this stage, you have addressed the challenge of Product/Market Fit: You have built something customers want, something they use, and something they happily recommend to others. Also, you've probably cut corners in many ways to get confirmation as early as possible that you are heading in the right direction.

Riina Einberg, general manager at Taxify, sits in a comfortable chair in a trendy, industrial-looking (but temporary) office in Tallinn, Estonia, talking about her experiences with multiple Estonian startups.

> *I'm not a CFO or accountant, but I have done plenty of financial work and have always tried to figure out simple enough solutions for startups because if you engage financial experts too early, they tend to overdo it with their processes.*
>
> *In the early stages, the company is usually changing very fast. So, the business needs someone who says, "Okay, let's do what's enough for the current stage, and let's prepare a little bit for the next stage. At some point, maybe we need someone who does this financial stuff full-time and more professionally. But currently, this is enough. We deal with just this part and we leave the rest for later." This has been my role in Finance, HR, IT, and Office Management.*
>
> *Riina Einberg, general manager at Taxify, Tallinn, Estonia*

It is common knowledge in the startup scene that many startups fail because they scale up too early. It's not enough to know that your product is a success and that there is a big market for it. Before shifting up to the Acceleration level, you first need to improve the quality of your processes. As long as you were searching for business validation, you probably had manual accounting and management systems. You spent more time on customer service than on quality control. And most likely, you didn't spend much time on marketing plans and partner channels while you were still validating your product and talking with all customers personally. As Riina Einberg said, you cut corners and do the least amount that is necessary at the current level, with just a bit of planning ahead for the next level. Anything more is a waste of your time.

In the **Stabilization stage (5)**, the small child grows into a big child, but it's not ready to go to high school until it knows how to take care of itself. Your startup spends time fixing the holes in its processes. It's not ready for scaling up when the foundation is unfinished. You work on the challenge of Business/Market Fit: going through the remaining unvalidated hypotheses concerning customer channels, business partnerships, and other parts of your business model. And you must delegate work to a qualified management team that knows how to scale up a business while at the same time getting funding to pay for the acceleration stage, possibly in a so-called Series A round, led by venture capitalists.

The Validation and Stabilization levels are together often referred to as Customer Validation. They are the early and late childhood stages of your startup. At these two levels, experimentation and learning are all about exploring the world and understanding the options. It is the part of the lifecycle where you first build a product that many people want, and test whether the business model is repeatable, profitable, and scalable.

It makes sense to distinguish two separate stages for Product/Market Fit and Business/Market Fit. In the Validation stage, you do things that don't scale, and you cut corners while validating the most essential hypotheses about your product. In the Stabilization stage, you fix the things that aren't scalable and get your business model ready to become a scaleup. Many founders, entrepreneurs, and intrapreneurs find it difficult to make this distinction because most startup literature treats Customer Validation and Product/Market Fit as one stage and then forgets about Business/Market Fit. But young kids and older kids play by different rules. You don't need a scalable organization until you have a proven product. Trying to make things scalable before knowing that your product works is not a smart thing to do.

The Stabilization stage is the last one where the business is still treated as a startup. From the next stage, we consider it to be a scaleup. It leaves its childhood years behind and shifts up into the world of grownups.

Paul Dolman-Darrall, CEO of Gamevy, explained in his small office in central London how his company struggled for three years and then suddenly found itself pulled into scaling mode.

Our mindset of "don't spend money" has switched to "spend it." Spend it sensibly but spend it. Don't slow the company down. Focus less on money and focus more on time. I think that's a big switch in our thinking that happened between surviving and scaling. Surviving was about not spending money at all costs. Now that we started scaling, it's about not wasting time at all costs. Because now time is the thing that could kill us as opposed to money.

Paul Dolman-Darrall, CEO of Gamevy, London, United Kingdom

The **Acceleration stage (6)**, sometimes referred to as Customer Creation, is the point where the balance tips from exploration to execution. The kid is an adolescent now. Its experimentation and learning are now more focused on how to be successful in the future.

Once your startup has done all the work of validating Product/Market Fit and Business/Market Fit, it is easy for competitors to simply copy what you're doing. This means that your business has to shift into a higher gear. From this stage onward, you try all you can to prevent being outcompeted, which is a common reason for business failure.

A business model that is scaling up has its focus on growth in revenue and market share. It has found a consistent source of income, but it may still struggle to make it sustainable and cash-flow positive. The challenge for the business is to reach more and more customers with a product that works while not overreaching what the business is capable of handling. Additional funding is likely needed while scaling, which is then often referred to as a Series B round.

For business leaders at this level, it is a challenge to deal with a whole new range of demands that require their attention, which includes recruitment, competition, partnerships, and organizational culture. The business replaces its informal learning team with a more formal structure, possibly with sales and marketing, business development, product development, and a bunch of executives managing everything. A lot of attention goes into optimizing, delegating, automating, evolving, and outsourcing the business processes.

At some point at this adolescent level, we say that the kid has become a young adult and therefore it gets the same rights and duties as the other adults in the family. It is now expected to play the rest of the game as a grown-up.

In the **Crystallization stage (7)**, your business is a young adult. It has successfully survived the challenging and exciting Acceleration stage—I suppose we all have special memories of our teenage years— and you might see that the growth of sales is tapering off and perhaps becomes linear rather than exponential. Running the business becomes more routine. In this stage, it is easier than before to attract people and resources because of the company's track record with an established, crystal-clear business model. On the other hand, the original startup culture of the business has probably been mostly lost by this time. Those working on the business may feel that it is becoming just another regular, big organization.

At this seventh level, there is increased competition which means that the company has to spend time improving business processes to further increase productivity and efficiency. When the company needs additional funding, it likely starts a Series C round, usually led by equity firms and investment bankers, with the focus being mainly on improving profits and preparations for further expansion.

This is also the perfect time for the young adult to start generating some offspring, if it hasn't done so already as an adolescent. The established business model is best positioned to continue with its own lifecycle, while at the same time initiating and funding new ideas, which can then be managed as corporate startups.

The seventh stage is also the typical level at which the founders of a new business push for an IPO or a sale to a larger company. Only in rare cases do the original founders hang on to their business creations. They usually want to move on and, not uncommonly, start making new business babies elsewhere.

The **Expansion stage (8)** is where the business model experiences its midlife crisis. It starts to show clear signs of aging and the business tries different things to stay dynamic and youthful. It funds new ideas through internal startups, adds new products and services to its existing markets, and brings more variety to its product line. It also attempts to bring its established, profitable business model into new distribution channels and new markets. In short, it travels a lot and tries anything to stay relevant.

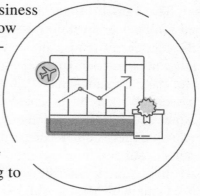

However, the competition does not sit still, either. Without a constant need to adapt and expand, complacency may set in. The market has seen the successes of the business and is actively co-opting its ideas, often in more interesting ways. A decline of the business is inevitable once it stops making room for innovative new ideas.

I think it's important to emphasize that, while the company as a whole could be getting larger, individual products and services within the company should be treated as being in different stages of their Business Lifecycle. Some business models are still babies; others are toddlers, kids, or teenagers. The adults usually pay for everything, including the care of the elderly. The organization is a family that tries to stick together and thrive through ongoing renewal. The only way for a family to survive the passage of time is to keep making babies. The only way for an organization to survive is to keep generating new businesses.

No matter whether a business model still stands on its own or is part of a larger company, the **Conservation stage (9)** is the point where atrophy sets in. It is the beginning of the end for your business model. Customers are moving elsewhere, sales and profits are dropping, and there could be a negative cash flow. The business is now a senior citizen, with an eye on a retirement home.

Despite having enjoyed a dominant position in the market, the organization is mostly concerned with cutting costs and putting most of its energy into younger, alternative business models. It will help sustain the current one for as long as is reasonable, but it will expect the business model to collapse at some point. Euthanasia is sometimes an option.

The **Finish stage (10)** is where the typical business model lifecycle comes to an end. If you were the founder of the business, you probably already have enjoyed your personal exit in an earlier stage. But the company's current leaders have to make a decision about the business that is about to end: either shut it down completely or break it up into valuable pieces and reuse them or sell them off to others. This might depend on the final wish of the terminal patient regarding organ and tissue donation.

I call these 10 stages the Shiftup Business Lifecycle and I feel the need to emphasize three important points. First, the lifecycle of a business is more flexible than that of a human being. To my great regret, physical constraints prevent the human body from reverting from middle age to the stage of young adulthood. But a business model is just an economic collaboration between people and shifting down to a lower level of the lifecycle is certainly possible. When the environment suddenly changes, a business model that had already been validated may have to be fixed and validated again. The aim is to reach and complete the higher levels of the game, but, occasionally, a business may be thrown back to a lower level. The lifecycle stages are not as discrete and linear as my descriptions make it seem.

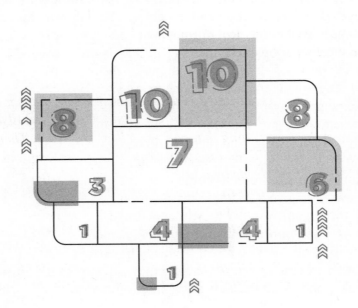

Second, as I've pointed out before, rather than seeing a whole company as existing in one specific stage, it is a fundamental shift in our thinking to assign lifecycle stages to its individual business models. When you have a startup, your company is practically synonymous with the business model. Therefore, the lifecycle stage of the business model is easily misinterpreted as the lifecycle stage of the company. But when your company scales up and establishes itself, you will probably launch new products and services with *different* business models. These new business models begin as just an idea, which means they start at level one. Like a family consisting of relatives in various stages of their lives, we should see companies as legal constructs wrapping businesses in different stages of the typical Business Lifecycle.

Third and last, there is not much difference between independent startups and corporate startups. To enable continuous innovation, established companies need to have teams that can explore new ideas and experiment with new business models. These teams should be treated and managed as internal startups. The way intrapreneurs should conceptualize ideas, test their hypotheses, and validate Product/ Market Fit is not really different from the way independent founders and entrepreneurs are learning to do that. The sequence of Initiation, Expedition, Formation, Validation, and Stabilization applies to every new business and different rules apply to different stages. American comedy series have generated many good laughs by showing children that act like adults. It's funny because it's ridiculous. Don't let your corporate startups become a joke. Allow them to be kids and allow them to fail safely.

I was in Espoo, Finland, at Rovio Entertainment, creator of Angry Birds, talking with Teemu Hämäläinen, product director and creator of several popular games.

In mobile games production, the big picture has different phases. It all starts in the creative phase, which is about concepts and ideas for a product. You are very small. You make something fun but you also keep in mind that you make something that can grow over the years. Then, after you've built and validated the prototype, you grow your team size and your adaptation speed drops by a half. Typically, in the production phase, your core team size is between 10 and 20 people. With that team, you're going to implement your product so that you can test launch it in a test market. So, you put it out in the marketplace, but you have it available only in maybe one territory. You now have real users playing your game but your adaptation speed drops to half once again because you have a live product to operate and users to take care of. But now you can also

start gathering real metrics. How do players really behave in your game? How do they stay there? Do they monetize in there or do they get stuck somewhere? Once again, you're learning and adapting, but the rate slows down over time. And this same lifecycle applies to each and every game.
Teemu Hämäläinen, product director at Rovio Entertainment, Espoo, Finland

The three phases that Teemu mentioned are a summary of the stages that apply to almost every game, every business model, and every startup idea. The best founders, entrepreneurs, intrapreneurs, and business leaders figure out how to do the right things at the right time, starting with exploration and steadily tipping the balance toward execution.

It is what I told my team members after I experimented with some early prototypes at the Expedition level and then decided to shift the business up to the Formation level by self-funding my startup and hiring a full-time team. I told them where I wanted to end up: organizational change empowered with a gamified platform and machine learning. I also told them I had no idea how to get there. And like a bunch of inquisitive toddlers, we started exploring.

For related notes, articles, books, examples, and downloads, check out this web page: https://startup-scaleup-screwup.com/business-lifecycle.

Picking Up the Pieces

Make a Business Quilt by remixing the Lean Canvas and Business Model Canvas and adding a dimension of time.

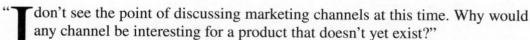

"I don't see the point of discussing marketing channels at this time. Why would any channel be interesting for a product that doesn't yet exist?"

I was discussing our business model with my new remote team in an online video meeting. Over a period of two months, I had hired all seven team members through my mailing list and word-of-mouth. My hiring process was ad-hoc and improvised, but it got the job done. I actually managed to hire good people and, with some difficulty, rejected all applications from crackpots, corpses, and kangaroos.

Using my own money, I formally launched the company, signed agreements, and thus transitioned from Expedition (2) to Formation (3) in the Shiftup Business Lifecycle. With my new team, I debated how not to screw up our new business, as I had done with some of my earlier startup ideas.

Nearly 20 years ago, during the infamous dot-com bubble at the end of the 1990s, I wrote a 40-page business plan for my first startup. It looked amazing. It showed diagrams of revenues going up, profits going up, company size going up, and my ego going up. All trend lines stood erect. It was a tantalizing sight that pleased the jury of a business plan award who made me Entrepreneur of the Year in The Netherlands in 1999. Sadly, the people who bestowed this title on me had even less experience running startups than I had, and we had no idea of what was coming. Three months after I had been beaming in front of the cameras, with the award in my hands, the dot-com bubble burst. My little venture sunk into oblivion not long after because the business model didn't work. I shelved my business plan as my first work of fiction. They might as well have named me Fantasy Writer of the Year.

One of the main reasons for startups screwing up is that they don't have working business models. Sometimes, it's an unwilling market; sometimes, it's monetization issues; sometimes, it's a rapidly changing environment. Very often, it's naivety and unpreparedness of the founders. The result is always the same. Despite great ideas, fabulous awards, and best intentions, the business model doesn't work. With my current venture, I feel motivated to do all I can to prevent that from happening to me again. Even if I must write an entire book just to learn more and increase my chances, I'll do that.

Unlike the startups of 20 years ago, the smart business creators of today don't write 40-page business plans anymore. Instead, they draw a Business Model Canvas (Figure 3.1, a tool proposed by business theorist and author Alexander Osterwalder) or a Lean Canvas (Figure 3.2, an adaptation offered by consultant and author Ash Maurya). Both models are well-known strategic tools that help people to document new and existing business models. These visual tools enable teams to sketch a complete business strategy by filling in a small number of boxes corresponding to different areas of a business model.

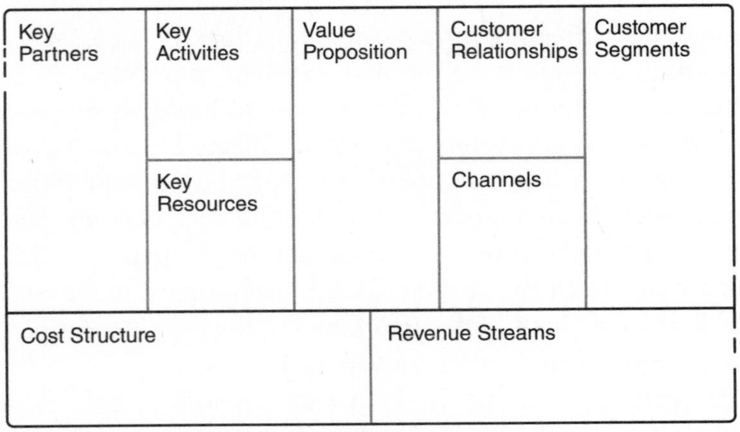

Key Partners	Key Activities	Value Proposition	Customer Relationships	Customer Segments
	Key Resources		Channels	
Cost Structure		Revenue Streams		

FIGURE 3.1 Business Model Canvas
Source: https://strategyzer.com/canvas/business-model-canvas; ShareAlike 3.0 Unported (CC BY-SA 3.0).

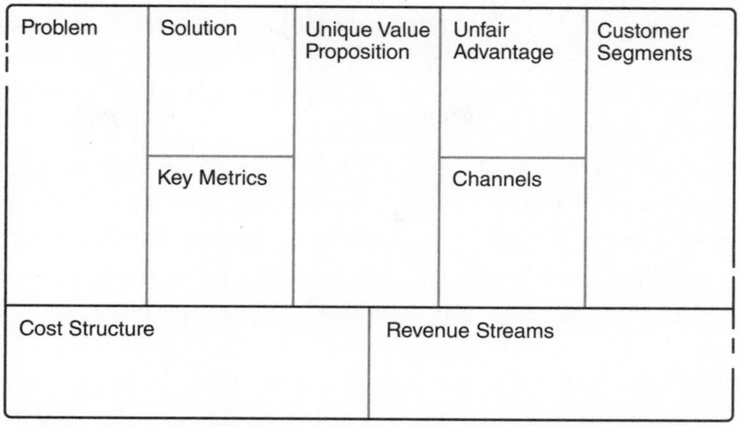

Problem	Solution	Unique Value Proposition	Unfair Advantage	Customer Segments
	Key Metrics		Channels	
Cost Structure			Revenue Streams	

FIGURE 3.2   Lean Canvas
Source: https://leanstack.com/leancanvas;
ShareAlike 3.0 Unported (CC BY-SA 3.0).

That's why I was poring over a Lean Canvas with my new team members, trying to discuss boxes such as Customer Segments, Problem, and Unique Value Proposition. I didn't want another business failure. This time, we would do everything right! But my team and I struggled to apply the canvas concept. It seemed to us that it was too early to discuss some boxes, such as Channels and Key Metrics, which meant we couldn't complete the picture. There was also confusion around the best order of filling in the boxes, with conflicting suggestions offered in various books and articles. Also, the positions of some boxes seemed arbitrary and we believed that some important topics were missing.

It seems to me there is something problematic about the canvas metaphor. By visualizing business model areas as a fixed, predefined template on one page, people get lost in discussions about the specific position and order of the boxes and whether some of them should be replaced with alternatives (as several authors have done). I think these are non-value adding meta-discussions and they distract a startup team from what really matters: designing a business model that works.

The canvas templates may also lead some people to believe that they can create an entire business model in one afternoon (or in less than 20 minutes, as one site suggests). But business strategy is an activity that never ends. A business model should be alive and growing, not remain static on a canvas. With our insights into the Business Lifecycle, we can easily see that, for the various business model areas, a temporal arrangement could be more interesting than a spatial arrangement. In our ongoing discussions about business strategy, which lifecycle level is the best place to discuss which areas? Where in the Business Lifecycle should we consider one topic done and start discussing another?

There is nothing wrong with the 13 business model areas covered by the Business Model Canvas and the Lean Canvas. But we can come up with many more interesting topics. In fact, the popularity of the original Business Model Canvas has caused an outbreak of alternative canvases for specific niches, of which the Lean Canvas is the best known to me because it specifically targets startups.

I believe we should be flexible about the number of business model areas and instead figure out which of them are going to be relevant in which stages of the Business Lifecycle. By starting with just one or two pieces, and gradually adding more pieces when it makes sense, you can patch together your own business model out of many different colorful topics. I call that approach the Shiftup Business Quilt (Figure 3.3). By using the metaphor of a quilt, we don't squeeze your business into a black and white template. Instead, we make it a colorful work of art and craftsmanship.

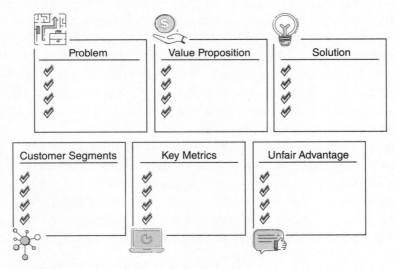

FIGURE 3.3   The Shiftup Business Quilt

Let's have a look at some relevant quilt pieces and figure out when to deal with them.

You can have no working business model without a **Problem/Opportunity**. You must be able to explain, to yourself, to customers, and to investors, which problem you will solve or which opportunity you will address. What are people's top frustrations or aspirations? What is their Job to Be Done (see Chapters 4 and 5)? What is the major Pain or irresistible Gain, and why are current solutions inadequate? The Problem/Opportunity topic is for many startups the first piece of their Business Quilt. You will probably discuss it from Initiation (1) at least until Formation (3) in the Business Lifecycle.

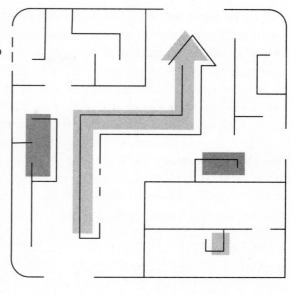

Sadly, founders and entrepreneurs tend to come up with solutions for problems that don't exist and, as I have done before, they screw up by building products that nobody wants. In the beginning, investors and customers don't care about your solutions. They only see problems and opportunities. You waste your time when you offer a solution that nobody wants or cares about. Therefore, as the first piece of your Business Quilt, define the problem or opportunity.

When you have an idea about a problem or opportunity, you will want to discuss **Customer Segments** or Target Markets. Who might be willing to pay for a new product or service? What are the demographics of your preferred customers? Do they have certain roles, traits, or habits? Can you describe them as Lean Personas (see Chapter 4)? Can you segment various sets of customers by identifying and clustering different needs, desires, and attributes?

Your customer segments and launch strategy are likely to evolve over time. Successful startups first sell to small groups of innovators and early adopters who buy a Product Vision, not a specific product version. Such startups keep segmenting the market until they have identified a customer profile they can win over with the vision of a new product. With the feedback from this first handful of innovative customers, they then add features over time to address bigger and bigger customer segments. The first version of your solution is not going to satisfy mainstream customers, but your later versions will. Logically, this means that the Customer Segments piece of your Business Quilt keeps evolving, from Expedition (2) at least until Crystallization (7) in your Business Lifecycle.

Nick Bortot, CEO and founder of the stock trading app BUX, was sitting at one of the company's lunch tables with me, in their office in Amsterdam. We enjoyed a super-healthy lunch meal, prepared by their in-house cooks.

We went live in Holland and three months later in the UK. Basically, right from the start, our idea was always to be pan-European and maybe even broader. But we learned an important lesson. In hindsight, we shouldn't have expanded to the UK so early. We should have focused on Holland first. We're Dutch. It's a small country, so it's great to do some testing here first. And once you see some traction, then branch out to other territories. Our go-to-market strategy could have been better.
Nick Bortot, CEO and founder of BUX, Amsterdam, The Netherlands

Together with Customer Segments, you will probably want to discuss your **Unique Value Proposition**. Each target audience has different objectives with different Pains and Gains. You must be able to explain to yourself and others what the value is of your offering. You need a narrative. Do you focus on performance, price, design, usability, convenience, or something else? What will make your solution different and compelling for your customers? Why would people buy from you and not from your

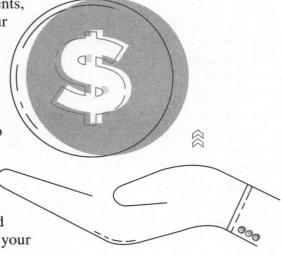

competitors? The creation of a Value Proposition Wheel (see Chapter 5) can help you out here. And similar to Customer Segments, the Unique Value Proposition piece of your Business Quilt is likely to evolve over time.

So, what are you going to do about that problem or opportunity? What will your **Solution** look like, considering the Customer Segments and Unique Value Proposition that you've identified? Can you describe the nature of your product or service in a concise and non-technical way? What is the type of your solution? Is it an app, a website, or a physical product? What does it do? In what experience category do you want your customers to place it so that they understand what it is? This might be a good moment to refine and share your Product Vision.

Assuming that you are an enthusiastic founder, entrepreneur, business leader, or creative, like many other people I know, I expect that you have already been tinkering with a Solution and Product Vision since you were thinking about the Problem/Opportunity in the Initiation stage (1). There's nothing wrong with that. However, the tinkering will have to continue for as long as you're learning new things about Customer Segments and Unique Value Proposition, probably all the way to the Crystallization stage (7). Your Solution piece will keep evolving with your insights about the market.

When you have ideas about who will want your product, and why, you can think about the desirable **Revenue Streams**. How are you going to make money? What will be the financial model of your business? Will there be a subscription fee, or will you earn a fee per transaction? Will there be a freemium service? And is the model going to be different per target audience? Similar to the Customer Segments and Unique Value Proposition, your Revenue Streams can evolve over time, either for strategic reasons, or because you pivot away from a model that doesn't seem to work. I expect that this piece of your Business Quilt is one of your main concerns from the Validation stage (4) up until the Crystallization stage (7).

An interesting topic that comes up frequently among startups is when to start charging their customers. In my research across the world, I encountered two philosophies that seem to be at odds with each other. The first says that it's a mistake to give away or heavily discount early versions of a solution because innovators and early adopters are happy to pay for early access to something new. If they don't want to pay yet, they are not your target audience. Testing which revenue model works and validating the willingness of customers to pay for your product, should be an essential part of your business strategy. Paying customers also give better feedback than users who get everything for free. Plus, when people have free access to it, you might be framing your solution as having no intrinsic value. It will then be much harder to add a price tag later. When you intend to charge customers for a product, it's best to charge them from day one.

However, some startup founders and entrepreneurs follow a different philosophy. They say it's possible to scale up first and then charge customers later. In the case of multi-sided platforms, the size of the user base can help such businesses attract paying customers who won't join their platforms as long as they are still small. This approach is not really in conflict with the first philosophy because the choice made here is to defer monetization until different customer segments can be added later. For some paying customers, a large scale is a prerequisite. Being the first one to capture a full market space can be essential for later revenues.

Michał Borkowski, founder and CEO of Brainly, based in Kraków, Poland, shared the following insights in telling me a few things about his business model strategy.

> It was a strategic decision not to monetize from the start. I got a lot of advice to do it differently. But there was the question, do we monetize in Poland, or are we trying to go after a global opportunity? I think we've made the right decision because we've proven that we can build an educational company that helps students on a global scale. The problem with monetizing only in Poland was that it's not like you launch one

feature and then it's going to work. You need to have an idea about how to monetize. You need to have a strategy. You need to invest before making profits. But it takes like two or three years to really figure out how you're going to monetize. There are so many questions around monetization. And then you are in just one market. While you're working on traction and monetization, three years pass by, and it's too late to scale out to the rest of the world. That was the problem that I was afraid of. That it would be too late for us to go international. That's why we decided to scale out to new markets first, finance that growth with funding, and then tackle the monetization later.

Michał Borkowski, founder and CEO of Brainly, Kraków, Poland

Besides the Revenue Streams explaining how you will earn money, your **Cost Structure** is the other financial piece of your Business Quilt. For many companies these days, the biggest expense is people. That much is obvious. But are there any other operational expenses? What will be driving your customer acquisition costs? What will be your monthly burn rate?

It makes sense to me to already address costs from the Formation stage (3) in the Business Lifecycle. After all, costs often precede revenues, and limiting the burn rate is one of the most important challenges for founders in the early stages of their business. You will have costs launching your company and hiring the first team members even before you can discuss the Revenue Streams piece with them. From that point onward, both costs and revenues are highly relevant because unresolved pricing/cost issues are among the top reasons that startups fail.

When the first customers are using your product, you will start accumulating data and you can focus on your **Key Metrics**. What are your conversion rates and retention rates? How do you validate that you're offering value for your customers (in the beginning) and how do you measure your growth rates (later)? What is your North Star Metric and what do the results of your Pirate Metrics look like? (These are tools to set objectives and measure progress; see Chapters 12 and 23.)

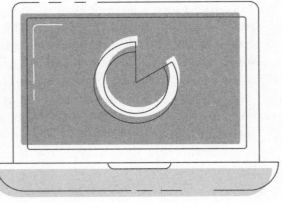

The key metrics for your business are another good example of an area of the business model that will change over time. As long as you're still exploring, usage and retention are much more important to scrutinize and optimize than conversion and revenue. Later, when you're preparing to scale up, you will probably be more interested in customer acquisition costs and customer lifetime value. Again, the pieces that you add to your Business Quilt depend on the lifecycle stage of your business and are likely to change over time.

An interesting thing to consider at some point is what **Unfair Advantage** you have over competitors that will be extremely hard for them to overcome. This should preferably be something that cannot be copied or bought and that would take a considerable amount of time to replicate. What makes your business model hard to copy? Are you in a position to defend your business with intellectual property, celebrity status, a large client network, or some patented technologies? Do you excel at lean/agile processes which allows you to iterate much faster than others? Success is often first achieved by the first movers and then stolen by the fastest learners.

Investors, in particular, will want to know about your unfair advantage. That means it is a topic to discuss as early as the Validation stage (4) and it will probably keep being a point of concern until the Crystallization stage (7) or even longer.

How will customers become aware of your of-fering? Is it through a website, social media, third-party distributors, or some combination of those? Will you be advertising, cold calling, or will you rely on viral effects and word of mouth? All of these are important things to consider *before* scaling up, but *after* you know that your product works. If your solution doesn't work well, and your key metrics are not showing any impressive figures in terms of usage and retention, it probably makes little sense to add the **Channels** piece to your Business Quilt. Why would you spend time figuring out how to reach your intended customers when the customers don't like your product? I think channels and market strategy are a thing to focus on after validation of the product, from the Stabilization stage (5) and onward.

But wait, there's more!

Other business model areas to consider, as suggested by the Business Model Canvas, are **Customer Relationships**, **Key Partners**, **Key Activities**, and **Key Resources**. But I believe that, in many cases, adding these pieces to your Business Quilt can be postponed until the Stabilization stage (5) or even later. Take your time! There's no need to have a complete quilt when your business is still exploring.

Additionally, a simple Internet search for alternative canvases reveals that other authors define separate areas for topics such as **Jobs to Be Done**, **Market Size**, **Trends**, **Network**, **Culture**, **Intellectual Property**, **Company Purpose**, **Operational Strategy**, and many others. And when you check the Pitch Deck slides that investors like to see (discussed in Chapter 21), you will find additional topics such as **Product/Secret Sauce**, **Product Roadmap**, **Competition**, **Financials**, **Milestones**, and more. As you can see, your Business Quilt does not need to be constrained to the standard pieces defined by the two most popular canvases.

It's your business. Your quilt. Make the patchwork as diverse and colorful as you think is necessary. You get bonus points if you can make it look like a rainbow. Double points if the quilt has the form of a unicorn.

The main benefit of canvases and other visual tools is that discussions around business strategy are easier when the models are visualized on paper, or on a wall, and when participants use standard terminology that people agree on. However, two things led me to believe that it's better to change the metaphor from a canvas to a quilt.

First, the layout of the boxes on the canvases suggests that there are direct connections between certain areas. To some extent, this may be true. However, it is also true that, in business strategy, everything is somehow connected to everything else, and the fact that people create alternative canvases with different boxes and layouts indicates that they have different perspectives on how the business model areas should connect with each other. I don't believe that any of these perspectives is the best. They are all useful.

Second, from the many articles about business model canvases, it is evident that the relevance of the different areas changes over time, depending on the current stage in the Business Lifecycle. Understanding Customer Segments and Problem/ Opportunity usually comes before everything else, but areas such as Channels and Key Partners are relevant only much later. It makes sense to give up on the idea of fixed, predefined templates. I prefer that people pick only the pieces they believe are relevant at the moment, visualize them on paper, or on a wall, and then stitch them together like a quilt that will probably keep evolving.

On top of that, companies and their environments change all the time. Target audiences come and go; opportunities and partnerships appear and disappear; revenue streams that worked last year might stop working next year. All the more reason to see the visualization of your business model as something that will always keep changing. Like Donald Trump's opinion on almost anything.

The most important aspect of business strategy and business model design is to capture guesses and assumptions about how the business should work and then have those ideas *tested*. The boxes on a canvas, and the pieces of your quilt, are nothing more than categorized checklists of hypotheses that need to be validated. Once you realize that the items within those pieces have a *status* that starts with a half-baked idea and ends with validated learning, you realize that the pieces of the quilt can be used as categories for Lean Experiments that can be placed on a Kanban Board, so you can follow them to completion (see Chapter 8). Your Business Quilt is then the driving force behind capturing your riskiest assumptions and having them tested as soon as possible.

For now, I suggest you only pick the pieces that make sense to you *at this moment*, in the current stage of your Business Lifecycle, and patch them together in any layout. Ignore everything I said about Jobs to Be Done, Lean Personas, Value Proposition Wheel, North Star Metric, Pirate Metrics, Lean Experiments, Kanban Boards, and Pitch Decks. We will return to these tools soon enough. Just fill in the pieces with your best guesses and ideas. If you do this on a wall, you can discuss them collaboratively with your team, using sticky notes or board markers. Make a habit of revisiting your Shiftup Business Quilt every month or so, to see if pieces need to be added, removed, or repositioned, and to check which ideas within those pieces have been validated or rejected.

I've had many business model discussions with my team about Problem/Opportunity, Customer Segments, Unique Value Proposition, and Key Metrics. And of course, we discussed many times our proposed solution to achieve organizational change through machine learning and gamification. We made two important decisions early on. One was that we would create a simple working prototype of an app, on the Android platform only, that was so basic we were almost too embarrassed to show it to anyone. The other was that we insisted on charging every user a monthly fee, from day one, just to see if they would support our vision and to ensure that they give us critical feedback.

There's no guarantee that our extensive business model discussions will help us prevent failure with this venture. But I feel that my chance of success is now better than ever. Unlike the previous times, I'm much more aware of addressing the right areas at the right time. And just to be sure, I decline all invites for startup contests. There's no penalty for superstition.

> *Starting up a business is about falling on your face and standing up,*
> *repeatedly. A serial entrepreneur is a person who stands up at least*
> *one time more often than he falls. And that's also true for a successful*
> *founder because there are many, many screwups along the way, but you*
> *need to keep managing them and keep your true north. And so, I believe*
> *that perseverance and resilience are the top criteria to be looking for in*
> *founders and entrepreneurs.*
>
> *Marc Wesselink, managing partner at Startupbootcamp,*
> *Amsterdam, The Netherlands*

That's how Marc Wesselink, managing partner at Startupbootcamp, explained to me, in a cheery mood, how he had stood up every time after falling down. I just hope I will now remain standing.

For related notes, articles, books, examples, and downloads, check out this web page: https://startup-scaleup-screwup.com/business-quilt.

The Persona Protocol

Better understand your target customers and their Jobs to Be Done by creating Lean Personas.

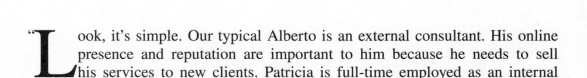

"Look, it's simple. Our typical Alberto is an external consultant. His online presence and reputation are important to him because he needs to sell his services to new clients. Patricia is full-time employed as an internal coach. She doesn't need an online profile; she just needs an updated CV when she switches jobs."

"Okay, but Alberto and Patricia are similar when it comes to scaling up their services. Our Albertos keep saying that they are overworked. They are asked to help too many teams. And our Patricias report the same thing: scaling up their coaching to more teams. Same problem."

"True. An important difference between Alberto and Patricia may be measuring the effect of their jobs. They would both like evidence that coaching and consultancy work. But this seems more important for Alberto, as a short-term contractor, than for Patricia, as a permanent employee."

And on and on it went. Our team was transitioning from the Formation stage (3) to the Validation stage (4) of the Shiftup Business Lifecycle. All legal and financial matters for the next half year were settled. The team had bought into my Product Vision and we were discussing our primary and secondary target audiences. We had defined them as Alberto, the External Consultant, and Patricia, the Internal Coach.

Alberto and Patricia don't really exist. They are Lean Personas, sometimes referred to as proto-personas or archetype users. Lean Personas are fictional but realistic characters that represent typical users of your product. As visualized abstractions, they make it easier for you to discuss your target audience and to identify their needs. Typically, a Lean Persona is a profile description that fits on one piece of paper, containing a photo, a name, sometimes a quote, and then several fields with fictitious personal data showing everything that is relevant about your most typical customers (see Figure 4.1).

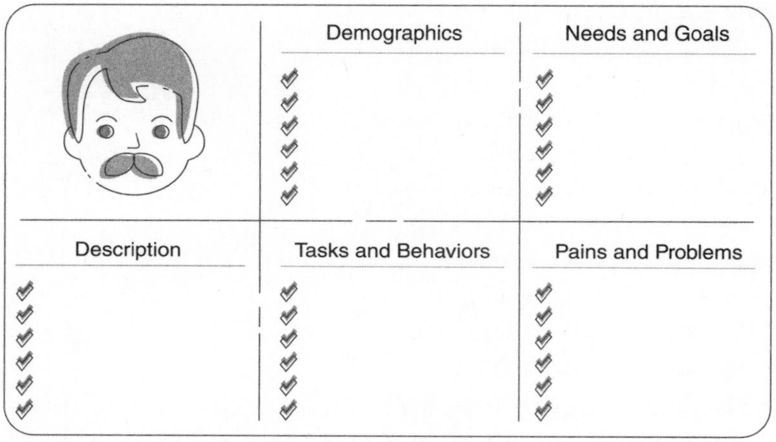

FIGURE 4.1   **Lean Persona example**

Personas were introduced into user experience design by software designer Alan Cooper as hypothetical archetypes of actual users. The word *persona* comes from the Latin word for "theatrical mask." The user persona concept then became so popular that some designers went completely overboard with elaborate descriptions of their archetypes. For that reason, some authors, including me, prefer to use the prefix *lean* to remind everyone to keep the descriptions simple. You're creating a profile; you're not writing a biography.

Obviously, the archetype user is an exemplary picture. No actual person will fit the profile description exactly. The Lean Persona is supposed to be a representative across a customer segment and it should be the result of your investment in *empathy*, a crucial stream in the Shiftup Innovation Vortex (see Chapter 9).

A Lean Persona helps you understand a target audience like a photo album helps you understand your family-in-law.

One or two centuries ago, when I was still young, it was normal to expect customers to read a user manual before using a new product. In fact, I didn't even want to turn on my new portable cassette recorder, electronic typewriter, or scientific calculator before I had a chance to read the manual. But those days are long gone. When was the last time you read a user manual? I bet it was ages ago. Nowadays, customers expect products to be simple to use and easy to understand. The user experience of new products needs to be top-notch or else users aren't even going to bother. By using Lean Personas, you can increase your understanding of what customers will expect from you.

Traditionally, target audiences are often defined using demographics, such as gender, ethnicity, age, education, income level, marital status, and so on. "Our target audience consists of unmarried, Latin-American women, 25 to 35 years old, with a college degree, and an income between 50K and 75K," or something like that. Such statistical information can be useful when you select publications and distribution channels for traditional advertising. But demographics are useless in product and service design. It would be hard for our team to identify the needs and desires of 25- to 45-year-old mostly white professionals in Europe and North-America. It is much easier for us to empathize with Alberto and Patricia.

Understanding the needs and desires of your typical target users is crucial for your team to make better design decisions. Lean Personas offer a narrative that is visual, memorable, and understandable, increasing the chance that you keep the right people in mind during product strategy, design, development, and customer acquisition. You don't want to waste effort creating features that nobody wants. You don't want to waste time writing a manual that nobody reads. What you want is to make sure that the focus of your team is on creating value, on solving a problem for someone. And that person for whom you are solving a problem could be very different from yourself, which means you need a way to empathize with them. Lean Personas enable you to do exactly that.

Personas are purely fictional, like easy exits out of the European Union, and easy entries into the United States. However, the target audiences that personas represent are discovered, not invented. The only way to empathize with customers is, as entrepreneur Steve Blank says, to Get Out of the Building and interview many people who are part of your target audience. Business consultant and academic Clayton Christensen says that your objective is to understand people's Jobs to Be Done. What is the thing that your intended customers need to accomplish? What are their primary needs and desires? By iteratively developing Lean Personas that represent your users, you will be able to get a deeper understanding of the problems and opportunities to be addressed with your product.

Typically, your Lean Persona descriptions start with a number of unvalidated ideas and assumptions about your target users. Your job is to use customer interviews, user surveys, field studies, observations, helpdesk analysis, and other techniques to replace more and more of your assumptions with real evidence. The more you research, the less you will be biased toward your own preferred solution.

When you get a deeper understanding of your target audience, you might notice some important differences between people. You can emphasize those differences by creating multiple personas that your team can then discuss and prioritize. My team members ended up with more than 40 personas before I threatened to take away their keyboards and kill 5 of them. (I meant personas, not team members.)

No matter how many you have, it will be useful for your team to have just one *primary* persona. Design and develop your product with just *one* ideal user in mind because a product designed for multiple, different typical users at the same time will be perfect for nobody. However, you can use secondary and tertiary personas to increase the likelihood that your product will also appeal to others (without compromising on design decisions for your primary persona) and, if needed, offer alternative interfaces or access points for the other target users. Focus on one and be inclusive toward others.

Working with multiple personas and target audiences can sometimes be a bit of a challenge to explain to others, which is usually the case when you're creating a product with a multi-sided market. In the Customer Segments piece of your Business Quilt, and on the Target Market slide of your Pitch Deck, you will need to explain what the complete market is that you hope to address over time. But listing 40 different personas is not going to be useful to outside stakeholders. So, you may have to condense the information and summarize it for others.

When you have prioritized your Lean Personas, it is much easier for your team to get alignment on the Value Proposition Wheel, which paints a picture of how you will make the target audience happy, and the Lean Experiments that you will have to perform to check if your business model is working for that audience. We will discuss these tools soon. Team roles in management, design, development, marketing, and customer service all need a shared understanding of the target user and how to address their needs.

Rickard Svedenmark, chief technical officer (CTO), shared stories with me about fishing, at the office of Fishbrain in Stockholm, Sweden.

> *It differs a lot between our different types of users. Some users are very interested in just getting the social engagement and recognition from others. They want to brag about their catch. Some post pictures and thrive off of the social recognition, the Likes, and the comments. And then there are others who don't care about that. They only want the tools that we offer. One of our users is traveling around all states in the United States and has dedicated his life to catching as many different species as he can. He bought an RV. He has a kayak on the roof, and then he goes to new places all the time. For him, actually being able to understand what fish is in a new water, and finding that fish, is the big value for him. He is not driven by the social aspect of fishing but by the tools and insights we offer.*
> *Rickard Svedenmark, CTO at Fishbrain, Stockholm, Sweden*

Rickard told me he didn't actually document the different types of users as Lean Personas, but he knew their different user types well. The goal is to *understand* your customers, not to *formalize* them. So, don't go overboard on the documentation side.

Keep your Lean Personas lightweight by constraining their descriptions to not more than one page with a small set of variables. If the need of your target user is to make an amazing coffee at home in under three minutes with a fancy espresso machine, your target customers' age, height, and skin color are irrelevant, but their location and financial position could be decisive. This is where many standard templates for Lean Personas fail because they suggest that you fill out a fixed set of variables that, in many cases, have zero relevance to your product or service.

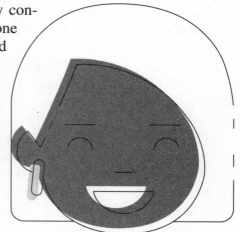

When you keep your Lean Personas lightweight, it will also be easier for you to change them later. The more extensive the research is on the development of personas, the more these descriptions become *untouchable* because of all the effort that went into creating them. Rather than spending months interviewing people, spend just an hour or two on initial descriptions and then start iterating on a monthly basis. Markets and target audiences change over time, and so will your personas. Be prepared to revisit and update them regularly.

Twenty years ago, I screwed up my first startup because I had no idea who my customers were. I had zero target audiences. Well, maybe I had one: me. This time, with more than 40 Lean Personas, my team has too many. The temptation to prioritize some over others, just because they show an interest in what you're doing, is high. We wasted many hours on Jane the Enterprise User because some of my business contacts wanted to know more about our startup and we saw an opportunity to sell our product idea to large corporations. But it turned out to be far too early for such big business partnerships. As a small team that barely emerged out of the Formation stage (3), we were absolutely not ready to address the needs and desires of enterprise clients. Our subsequent decision to stick to Alberto and Patricia, our two prioritized Lean Personas, prevented another major screwup.

For related notes, articles, books, examples, and downloads, check out this web page: https://startup-scaleup-screwup.com/lean-personas.

Fortune's Wheel

Figure out your Unique Value Proposition by investigating the customer's Pains and Gains and making a Value Proposition Wheel.

I remember exactly when and where I had the insight. I was enjoying a 12-kilometer run in London along the 4 Pound Path, which proves to me that running is a great way to clear the mind and have new insights. On this sunny morning in spring, I was thinking about the value that my team wanted to offer to our customers and it occurred to me that something essential was missing from our value proposition.

Our startup had arrived in the Validation stage (4) of the Shiftup Business Lifecycle. It is the level at which startups begin working to find Product/Market Fit: a good match between a new product and a large market that wants it. Some experts say finding Product/Market Fit is the toughest challenge for any startup. And my team was feeling that, too. We had a prototype that worked for some, but it was not interesting enough for most. We had scored our first paying customers, but we were still far from good monthly revenues. It was like offering a solar-powered bicycle with a flat tire and no saddle. The innovators and adventurous-inclined were intrigued, but most people preferred to walk.

In the Validation stage, a startup keeps tweaking a new product's features and design until it can delight many customers in a promising market. Figuring out exactly what that product should do, and what it should look like, is extremely hard. It was, and still is, most certainly a challenge for us! If you thought raising children was difficult, try growing a few businesses. The survival rate of children is a lot better, and they ask for less money.

Let's go back to the beginning. Every startup needs to have a Product Vision, or purpose, and one or more Lean Personas, or customer segments. Why and for whom are you developing a product? To understand the value that you can offer to your customers, you first need to understand what they are trying to achieve. In other words, you study their Jobs to Be Done (JTBD). Are they trying to travel from A to B without any hassle? Are they trying to keep difficult projects on track? Do they need to talk to colleagues without interruptions? Don't limit yourself to their functional jobs, either. People also have things they want to achieve at social and emotional levels. Are they trying to find and meet new people? Do they want to be entertained at the click of a button? Do they need some time to relax and recover? In principle, your team should not start building any prototypes and solutions until they are well aware of the JTBD from the customer's point of view.

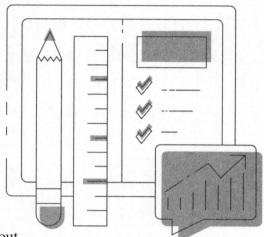

When examining people's needs and desires, you can distinguish between two types of value to offer: convenience (the relief of pains) and enjoyment (the creation of gains). Pains are the things that get in the way of people's JTBD. Pains make our customers' lives hard and frustrating. With our products, we have an opportunity to relieve those pains and make it more convenient for people to get their jobs done.

Gains are the things that would make JTBD more fulfilling. Gains make our customers happier. With our products, we have the opportunity to make it more enjoyable for people to get their jobs done. Offering taxi rides that require no cash payments is convenience (relief of pain). Offering taxi rides with a luxury old-timer is enjoyment (creation of gain). A free shuttle in a hotel limousine, a product that I've never been offered, would be both convenient and enjoyable. All products are offered to get the same job done: traveling from A to B.

In the case of my startup, the product that we're building is full of ideas for better work habits and practices. We know that Patricias and Albertos (our Lean Personas) have a need to *discover* interesting options for personal and team improvement; we know that they seek suggestions for *implementing* ideas from these options by acting out suggestions. We know that they want to *reflect* on what they experienced and evaluate the value created (or lost), and they want to *share* and make available the things that were learned as ideas for others. The learnings shared in this fourth part are input for new options in the first part, which neatly closes the circle. It looks like we could define what our customers are seeking as a flywheel of four parts. Every customer can pull on any part of this flywheel to make it go spinning. (See Figure 5.1.)

However, and this is what I realized when I was doing my morning run in London, at no point on this flywheel did my team and I know what our customers were actually *doing* in their day-to-day work lives. If we were more aware of their context, we would be much better able to offer suggestions, even when they're not actively searching for new ideas. After all, most people don't even realize that they can improve the way they do their work. And thus, I realized that we needed a way to make it valuable for users to share insights about their daily work lives with us. This sharing itself needed to be valuable for customers. Understanding what people are doing would be crucial to offering them better help.

Most businesses would like their users to develop a habit of using their products. For example, it is my habit to record my runs with Garmin. I find good restaurants and coffee places with Google Maps. And my daily rants about the

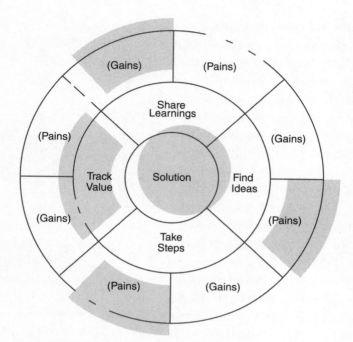

FIGURE 5.1 Value Proposition Wheel

universe, and how much it hates me, go on Twitter and Facebook. Similarly, my team is working hard to ensure that customers develop a habit of using our app to find and use better work practices. When creating habitual usage patterns, it is essential that you understand how your product delivers value to your customers. I believe that you can often visualize this as a flywheel.

In the case of simple products and services, there is usually just one obvious Job to Be Done, which makes it relatively easy to capture Pains and Gains. For example, I hate bad Internet connections. It's the worst crime after bad coffee. And the universe offers me plenty of both, because it hates me. That's why I recently bought Google Wi-Fi for my home. It sits not far from our espresso machine. Since installing this product, I have experienced not one single interrupted Wi-Fi connection, which is a major pain relief for me, and perhaps also for my neighbors. It has some other fancy features, but for me, Google Wi-Fi doesn't do anything interesting except stabilize my Wi-Fi. That's one job. An important one. However, in other situations, jobs are a bit more complicated. You might describe them as multiple, interconnected JTBD that, together, form a cohesive whole. In such cases, you can draw a value wheel.

Another example. I recently decided to switch from Google Contacts to Cloze, a contact management app. As an author, speaker, and entrepreneur, I am in contact with thousands of people and I need a decent way to organize all their contact information. My pain was that Google Contacts was extremely slow and limited to 25,000 contacts. (Yes, I have more than that.) The jobs that I need to get done are: combining contact information from multiple sources (such as LinkedIn connections, MailChimp newsletters, and company databases) so that everything is in one place, organizing (ranking and tagging) contacts so that I understand where they came from and how I got to know them, keeping track of contacts that I reached out to earlier so that I can follow-up on various statuses, and growing my network with new introductions so that the whole cycle can start again. This is not just one Job to Be Done. This is an entire wheel of Jobs to Be Done!

After my inspiring run in London, I made a drawing. I realized that our product could offer a flywheel of value by adding a missing piece in our offering. I worked on it throughout the weekend and discussed it with the team at an offsite in the following week. The visualization led to great discussions, a whole bunch of ideas for new product features, and it required me to update my original ideas about our Product Vision.

The Value Proposition Wheel can have two, three, four, or even more parts, and each spoke on the wheel can be one specific value proposition: a pain relief or a gain creation that you enable with your product. Each time your customer uses your product to relieve a pain or to enjoy a gain, it is as if they tug on the Value Proposition Wheel on that particular side. And every time, the customer can pull on a different side to experience a different benefit. If all goes well, the wheel starts spinning faster and faster.

Now, it's your turn. Find your customers' JTBD, identify the Pains and Gains, and then draw a Value Proposition Wheel. When the different parts of the wheel are all in place, it can act like a flywheel. The customer will appreciate your product for its multiple benefits that are all interrelated and that reinforce each other. Similar to operating a flywheel, it can take a lot of effort to overcome the initial inertia and get it started. But once the Value Proposition Wheel is spinning, it will take less effort to keep it humming along.

Keep in mind that the Value Proposition Wheel depends on the Lean Persona. When you pick a different target audience with different jobs they need to get done, you end up with another flywheel, maybe with a different number of parts. When you're building a product for a multi-sided market, it is likely that you will be needing a different Value Proposition Wheel for each customer segment. They might look alike, but there will certainly be important differences.

In Chapter 3, I briefly discussed the term *Unique Value Proposition* (UVP). A UVP is commonly a paragraph of one or two sentences that explains to your investors and employees what your business is offering. It is the promise of unique value to be communicated and delivered. A UVP helps your stakeholders to understand the primary focus of your business and the needs of your customers. Typically, the Unique Value Proposition is used by you as a founder, entrepreneur, or intrapreneur to explain why your offer is different from those of your competitors and why customers would choose you over others. For example, this is our team's UVP as included in our most recent Pitch Deck:

Business coaches and consultants worldwide need more than training, slide decks, and certificates to help companies be more agile. We offer a peer-to-peer advisory platform, with an app, that provides actionable ideas for change and evidence of improvement of the teams they assist and lead, all in one place.

When you compare the visualization of your Value Proposition Wheel and the description of your Unique Value Proposition, you can say that the UVP should be a written summary of the visual image. This is easy when you just offer one benefit with a simple product. It is a bit more challenging when your Value Proposition Wheel consists of multiple parts. In that case, you will have to be creative and take a higher-level view of the entire value wheel. Either way, when you use both techniques, make the results match.

Do *not* confuse UVPs with slogans, catchphrases, and Unique Selling Propositions (USPs), which are used by marketers in advertising to communicate the benefits of a product or service to customers. Obviously, a USP (or slogan or catchphrase) can be based on a UVP but it probably should use different wording that is specifically targeted at customers. It also tends to be a lot shorter. The intent of the UVP is to explain the business to investors and employees, while a slogan or USP explains a product to customers. UVPs are mainly used for internal communication; USPs are specifically used for external communication. For example, this is our team's slogan for our product:

The Agile Adventures Frontier

When you define your UVP as a paragraph of text, try not to enumerate a list of product features. Instead, describe how your product will make people's lives better by getting their jobs done with less pain and more gain. Different tools can help you with that. For example, there is the Value Proposition Canvas, offered by business theorist and author Alexander Osterwalder, and there are many value proposition templates, offered by other authors. Each of these helps you identify the essentials of your offering. I will leave it as a homework exercise for you to explore value proposition templates and canvases online and to experiment with them in combination with a Value Proposition Wheel. Both a Unique Value Proposition, as a text, and the Value Proposition Wheel, as a picture, can be important steps for you to take on the way to a product that is habitually used by your customers. Great fortune awaits those who offer great value.

Your insights from creating a Value Proposition Wheel can go straight into the Value Proposition piece of your Shiftup Business Quilt. For my team, the visualization of the flywheel has enabled us to better define our offering and to describe to our stakeholders what it is that we're doing. We've also decided to feature the wheel prominently in our next round of Equity Crowdfunding, which makes me realize that I haven't even told you about our first funding round. Shame on that part of the universe that I call *me*. Let's fix that oversight right now.

For related notes, articles, books, examples, and downloads, check out this web page: https://startup-scaleup-screwup.com/value-proposition-wheel.

The Crowded Shadows

Learn about the benefits of Equity Crowdfunding and choose between the use of a crowdfunding platform or doing it all yourself.

It was one of the most unnerving times of my life. The solid black line that I plotted on a piece of paper that showed how much funding the crowd had pledged to our startup was rising slowly but steadily. It was a weekly agonizing ritual to extrapolate that line to the day of the deadline and check whether it would end just above our minimum crowdfunding target, or just below it. Every week, I added the new investors. Every week, the line went up. Sometimes just a little; sometimes a little bit more. I can still see the bite marks on my coffee cup.

I've done many stupid things in my life but, occasionally, I pride myself on having done something smart, often unintentionally. On the stupid side of this rather unbalanced scale, we find the psychopaths who I dated and the money I invested in cryptocurrencies. On the smart side, we find the Special-Purpose Vehicle (SPV) that I set up with the notary at the time I launched our company. An SPV is a legal entity in which many investors can be pooled and, when the SPV owns shares in a business, it is represented as just one line on the capitalization table of the company. Future investors in the company will appreciate this construction because, rather than dealing with many small shareholders of a business, they will deal with just one, the SPV, which acts on behalf of dozens or even hundreds. (See Figure 6.1.)

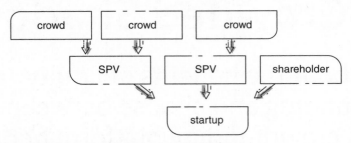

FIGURE 6.1 Special-Purpose Vehicles

In my country, The Netherlands, such an SPV is typically set up as a nonprofit foundation. The foundation owns shares on behalf of its investors and then issues certificates that confirm and validate that the shares in possession of the foundation are actually granted to its investors. Technicalities aside, the solution is pretty similar to the various legal constructions that accelerators and venture capitalists use to pool money from their own limited partners so that they can invest it in startups. It was my intention to use our foundation primarily to pool the shares of cofounders, advisors, and other business partners. I did not expect that the SPV would turn out to be a lifesaver at the end of our Equity Crowdfunding campaign.

Equity Crowdfunding is the online offering of ownership (with shares, certificates, or another type of securities) in a private company to a large group of people. Some of my sources claim that this type of funding now raises more money than traditional venture capital and that the market keeps growing with double digits each year. It seems inevitable to me that venture capitalists will go the same direction as travel agents, car dealers, and bookstores: extinction or specialization. For people with a small budget and an eye for margins, it makes sense to use apps and digital platforms rather than overpaid intermediaries with a cellphone and a secretary. Only investors with big budgets and specific needs will appreciate the services of the personalized broker between themselves and the businesses they invest in. The rest will move to platforms. Who still needs pimps, madams, and other agents when the market and the crowd have moved to Tinder, Happn, and Grindr?

Do not confuse Equity Crowdfunding with debt crowdfunding (borrowing money from a crowd and then paying it back with interest), which is also known as peer-to-peer lending (with Funding Circle and Flender as good examples). It is also not the same as product crowdfunding, which is asking a crowd to make down payments on the development of a new product in return for special privileges or exclusive versions (popularized by platforms such as Kickstarter and Indiegogo).

Equity Crowdfunding is about selling part of the ownership of your business in return for capital that is yours to keep and to spend. It works for all kinds of businesses, across all stages of their Business Lifecycle, but it's probably most often used by those in the Formation (3), Validation (4), and Stabilization (5) stages. The fact that you can combine Equity Crowdfunding with angel investors or venture capital makes the practice a very interesting component of an Agile Funding approach. It increases your options and reduces your dependency on specific sources of capital.

It was an easy decision for my team to use crowdfunding to fund our startup because of the number of people that were already familiar with my earlier work. The scene of angel funding and venture capital is quite opaque and requires a significant time investment in personal networking to raise people's interest and to get invites from investors. For those who are already well-connected with customers and business partners, such as yours truly, Equity Crowdfunding can be easier because, rather than asking a few people to invest large amounts, you ask many people to invest small amounts. This lowers the barrier of entry for young companies with good reputations. When our team worked on our Shiftup Business Quilt, they simply wrote my name on the Unfair Advantage piece, believing that the company would benefit from my network as a writer, speaker, and entrepreneur. This has certainly proven to be true for the crowdfunding.

There are even more benefits to getting financial support from a crowd. A successful round of Equity Crowdfunding means that you are able to convince customers and partners to not only buy and support your product but also to take a stake in its future, which is a positive signal for other investors. Vice versa, some of your small investors might consider becoming your customers too because they want your business to be successful. On top of such interesting spin-off effects, any crowdfunding that you do can raise awareness about your product in the media and among potential partners and employees, for free.

And with crowdfunding, you have access to your crowd of investors for feedback, ideas, and some warm connections to large customers and more investors.

What I like most particularly is that crowds don't come with complicating demands, such as preferential stock, a seat on the board of directors, a change in executive management, or a fat unicorn on a platter. The crowd remains in the shadows. For everyone in the crowd, there is just one set of terms to agree on, and these terms are pretty much standard across all crowdfunding campaigns and depend on your platform of choice.

Of course, there are some drawbacks, as well. Everything you do in an Equity Crowdfunding campaign will be public. If you fail your crowdfunding round, the world will see it. If you have an idea for an innovative new business model, remember that you are sharing it with everyone. If you ask the crowd to invest in a solar-powered submarine, they might talk about you for years. Also, depending on where your business is located, there may be a cap on the amount of money that you can raise from the crowd per year.

Last but not least, the crowd consists of many inexperienced investors. They have no idea what a proper valuation of the company would be. They ask newbie questions, such as, "How can I sell my shares?" (They can't, unless you or your crowdfunding platform organize a secondary market. Normally, investors just wait until the company is sold or goes public on a stock exchange.) This means that you need to be sure of what you're doing because your small investors won't help you prevent making bad decisions and some of them may need a bit of hand-holding.

There are two ways to organize a round of Equity Crowdfunding. You either do it yourself or you use a dedicated crowdfunding platform, such as Seedrs or Crowdcube. Crowdfunding platforms don't come free. The work that the platform owners do for you somehow needs to be compensated. As a fee, they usually ask between 5 and 8 percent of the funds that you raised. If that sounds like a lot, be aware that these platforms come with their own crowds. With the fee that you pay them, you purchase access to their network of crowd investors. What they also tell you is that they take work out of your hands, but I would challenge that.

Seedrs, the platform we picked to handle our Equity Crowdfunding, only handled European investors, but roughly a third of my network is outside of Europe. So, I decided to handle the non-European investors myself. We already had a foundation (the Special Purpose Vehicle) that could easily pool investors and offer them certificates. So, we created a new formal certificate agreement that bound company shares to crowd investors, through the SPV, in exchange for their funds. We created a sign-up page with our Pitch Deck, a Frequently Asked Questions page that covered all questions, a public folder with formal documents, and a newsletter to keep everyone updated regularly. And that was it. With a signature on a PDF document, we were then able to sell shares worth hundreds of thousands of euros. Official, legal, and simple.

What I just described is the do-it-yourself approach. Crowdfunding platforms such as Seedrs do all this work for you. They create their own Special Purpose Vehicle; they have their own help files for investors; and they have their own communication systems. However, in my experience, they also ask a lot of questions and require a mountain of legal documentation from the business just to get the whole campaign started and completed. All the time I spent satisfying the crowdfunding platform's insatiable need for information could easily rival the time I spent on the do-it-yourself crowdfunding approach with our foundation. In other words, I did twice the amount of work that I would have done had I chosen only one approach, rather than organizing it both ways. It felt like showing a real estate agent my house and explaining how to sell it, and then selling the house myself the very next day.

Did I mention a Pitch Deck? I'm sure I did. Aside from all the legal information, the FAQs, and the sign-up page, the Pitch Deck is the core of any funding campaign. You can (and should) create a video, and you can (and should) write blog posts, but everyone will expect you to have at least a Pitch Deck to flip through. Before our campaign started, we made sure to spend a lot of time creating and tweaking our presentation slides. We were still at the beginning of the Validation stage (4), which meant that we had only a limited prototype, with no gamification and no machine learning, and we had no meaningful revenues to show for. So, we mainly promoted the problem, our proposed solution, and the value proposition. Everything else was guesswork. (I will return to the topic of Pitch Decks in Chapter 21.)

And then, the marketing started. The amount of promotion you do will be the same, regardless of whether you use a crowdfunding platform or do it all yourself. The main difference is that all questions around legal issues will be addressed by the platform. More importantly, if you go your own way, you will not have access to the existing crowd on the platform and you need to be sure that you can find enough interested people in your own network. One final thing to consider is that there might be local, legal restrictions around promoting the sale of equity, even if it's your own company. Check with your financial advisor first!

The three months our crowdfunding campaign was running was a nerve-racking time for our team. With the Burn Chart (see Chapter 14) that I updated on a weekly basis, we could closely follow how much money investors had committed. After a few weeks, the chart showed an almost straight line going up that would barely reach our minimum target of 300K euros if extrapolated to the deadline.

For a long time, it was uncertain if we were going to make it. What would happen near the end of the campaign? Would the line go up faster when the deadline was coming near and would more and more of our fans experience a Fear of Missing Out? Or would the line start tapering off after we had exhausted all our network contacts and our friends would unfriend us because of the amount of spam we sent? We didn't know. If the campaign would not reach its minimum target, the entire funding round would be canceled, and all investors would get their money back. We would be out of business.

For related notes, articles, books, examples, and downloads, check out this web page: https://startup-scaleup-screwup.com/equity-crowdfunding.

The Lunatic Cafe

Meet every day with your team for a Daily Cafe and Work Out Loud by sending each other Daily Updates.

It was 17:00 (5 p.m.) Central European Time. I logged onto Zoom, our video-conferencing tool, and, one by one, my other team members came online. For about five minutes, we chatted about the FIFA World Cup finals and the heat wave that was smothering Northern Europe. I also told my team that my publisher asked me, for the third time, to write another book. As if my life as a startup founder wasn't busy enough already! Then it was time for us to spontaneously generate our meeting agenda. Three topics were typed into the chat window: some latest insights about our Value Proposition Wheel, our ongoing Equity Crowdfunding, and an idea to start reworking our Culture Code.

This time, it took 25 minutes to address the topics, which was above average for us. The team needed some time to discuss their concerns about the crowdfunding. I understood that. After all, it was unsure if we were going to make it, and if they all would still have a job two months later. At the end of the session, we did our usual Fist of Five to rate how valuable the meeting was. We were unanimous this time: a four out of five score from everyone.

The next morning, I wrote a Slack message to the team on our #work-out-loud channel so they would know what my plans were for the day:

"Today: Pay all monthly bills. Update the crowdfunding forecast. Travel to Berlin for a startup event. Have an argument with the universe."

I also informed the team that the travel meant I wouldn't be able to attend our Daily Cafe that day.

As a founder, entrepreneur, intrapreneur, and business leader, an important part of your job is to create an environment where people can easily communicate and collaborate. Without this, your team is not going to achieve much. Fortunately, some healthy team practices are quite simple to introduce and maintain.

For many professional software teams, a successful practice for communication and collaboration is the Daily Stand-up. It is a brief meeting, usually performed standing up for about 15 minutes, intended for the entire team to stay up-to-date on each other's progress, remind each other of important goals, coordinate work in an informal way, quickly identify problems and bottlenecks, and communicate topics that are best addressed face-to-face. The standard format for these meetings consists of three questions answered by every person on the team, in a peer-to-peer fashion:

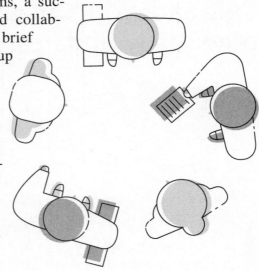

1. What did I accomplish yesterday/today (that helps us move forward)?
2. What will I do today/tomorrow (that will help us move forward)?
3. What obstacles are blocking my progress (or the progress of the team)?

Daily Stand-up meetings are successfully performed worldwide, but the introduction of this practice with startup teams and remote teams can be a challenge. There are experience reports suggesting that the Daily Stand-up practice doesn't work well with such teams. Startups and distributed teams need different ways of informing each other, different ways of making decisions, and different ways of staying connected. The nature of the work is more diverse, and the teams are more loosely coupled than in situations with collocated software teams. This leads to annoyance and impatience with the three standard questions. Why should the social media marketer tell the back-end developer about the e-mail campaign she was working on yesterday? Why would we assume that the user experience designer can help solve the technical problems that are reported by the app developer?

Another problem with Daily Stand-ups is the synchronization of status updates. Most remote teams are distributed across multiple time zones. Maybe it makes sense for someone to report their status to team members at 9:00 a.m. in New York. But for someone in India, the question "What will you do today?" is useless at 6:30 p.m. Quite often, remote teams see Daily Stand-ups as a waste of their time. The peer-to-peer updates are interesting, but people on distributed teams have recognized that asynchronous updates work just as well. Slack bots and other specialized tools ask team members 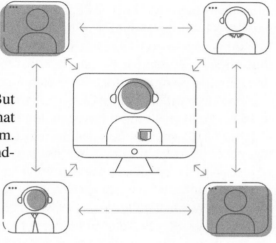 to inform their peers about their work-in-progress, at a time that makes sense in their own time zones, and this seems to work just as well and costs people much less time.

Sadly, because of the switch to asynchronous updates, many remote teams have ditched their daily meetings entirely, reserving their face-to-face discussions instead for weekly meetings. But that seems like a typical case of throwing out the baby with the bathwater.

Team members easily forget that get-togethers are not only about communication. Regular meetings are also about the social and complex aspects of team performance. With a remote team, the primary focus of daily meetings could be building relationships, straightening out the hard issues, and growing a great team culture. In other words, better collaboration. A daily face-to-face chat about two or three complex issues is an excellent way to bring a team closer together. Isn't that why friends and business partners meet for coffee or beer?

Some people would say that complex topics can be addressed spontaneously, in on-demand meetings. They would say there is usually no need to schedule a daily meeting with friends. This is true when it involves just two or three people and when any of them can easily text each other and say, "Hey, are you available today for a quick coffee? You pay this time." But try to organize spontaneous meetings with a group of four people or more and you're faced with scheduling issues, calendar clashes, and a huge loss of productivity.

It's much easier for you to have a dedicated Daily Cafe time slot reserved for anything that comes up. Once you have this, you will notice that team members will schedule fewer chats for three or four people because it's easier to bring up an issue in the next Daily Cafe. Your teammates can still choose not to attend this daily meeting if they prefer to focus on a critical issue instead, but the Daily Cafe functions as a strong nudge to socialize and talk about things that matter, and as a hint not to postpone such conversations for more than 24 hours. The objective of this meeting is for your team to collaborate.

On our team, the Daily Cafe is a chat about things that are best discussed face-to-face, briefly, between three or more people. We've decided to organize it at 17:00 (5 p.m.) CET, which means that, for most of us, it wraps up the day. Personally, I like that better than morning calls because any issue that comes up during the day can still be discussed the very same day, assuming that they don't need to be solved immediately.

By default, our entire team is invited for the Daily Cafes. But often, a few people don't show up because of holidays, personal errands, or occasionally because they already had too many meetings that day and just want to get some work done. The meetings always start on time and they are not postponed when a few people are not yet present.

Our Daily Cafes are very informal. Some of us like to join the meeting with a warm or cold drink in hand, a spouse in the background, or a cat or baby on their lap. It's even possible that someone is having dinner, as I once had when I was in transit at an airport. We once organized Formal Friday and showed up at the cafe in formal business suits and ties. The only thing I haven't seen among this bunch of lunatics is someone taking a shower.

After organizing these cafes a few hundred times, we've learned a few things to keep them valuable for us. On our team, we always start with a mandatory five-minute chit-chat because, as highly motivated professionals, we noticed that we had the tendency to immediately start discussing the important and complex topics. But we need to continuously remind ourselves that non-work-related conversations are also important for better team collaboration.

We don't send out agendas. We create a list of topics on the spot, at the last responsible moment. We type them into the chat window and then we work our way down the list.

It's good to have a timebox for Daily Cafes. For traditional Daily Stand-ups with regular teams, the common advice is a maximum of 15 minutes per day. But remote teams need a bit more time for team bonding, so we set our timebox to 30 minutes. Any meetings longer than that have a tendency for participants to become bored or distracted. Sometimes, our cafes take just a few minutes when only few team members show up and have little to discuss. Other times, it can take up to half an hour, which we stick to as our maximum.

There are usually three or four topics suggested for discussion, which take about 10 to 20 minutes to discuss in total. Anything big is delegated to fewer people in separate calls, whenever necessary. It's not uncommon for a team member to say to another, "Okay, let's hang around after the call to discuss the details." We are all conscious of not wasting everyone else's time.

It is good to have opening and closing rituals for your Daily Cafes. Our team developed the habit of giving every meeting a score at the end by holding up between one to five fingers (also called a Fist of Five) because we want to keep our cafes effective. A low score from any team member immediately creates awareness that there might be something about the meeting that we could improve. We take a screenshot of the votes and usually post it on Slack.

Now you might wonder when we tell each other, "This is what I did yesterday, and this is what I will be doing today." Well, we moved that part to our Daily Updates, on Slack, in our #work-out-loud channel.

Working Out Loud is an approach, promoted by author and entrepreneur John Stepper, that asks people to continuously share with their peers what they're doing and why. The idea is that, by broadcasting your intentions and whereabouts to those who are interested (most importantly, the team you're working with), it is easier for people to learn from what you do, reply with suggestions and improvements, and engage in collaboration.

Our team created a #work-out-loud Slack channel for our Daily Updates to which all team members are subscribed. Different teammates send updates at different times during the day, but most prefer sending them in the morning. Our different time zones, spanning from California to Poland, mean that the updates in this channel appear throughout the day. I read almost every one of them because I'm a curious person and I like knowing what's going on in the company. And I enjoy seeing that the things my teammates share are not exclusively limited to their work. I have no problems occasionally sharing some of my eating habits, running exercises, or books that I'm reading, and others are similarly open about the many things that are happening in their lives.

If you have an established, collocated team, it makes sense to combine peer-to-peer status updates with a daily meeting, which is the goal of the Daily Stand-up. But startup teams and remote teams benefit from separating out the face-to-face meetings, with Daily Cafes, from the working-out-loud approach, with Daily Updates.

For related notes, articles, books, examples, and downloads, check out this web page: https://startup-scaleup-screwup.com/daily-cafes.

Streams of Silver

Visualize your work with Kanban Boards and optimize the workflow with Work in Progress Limits.

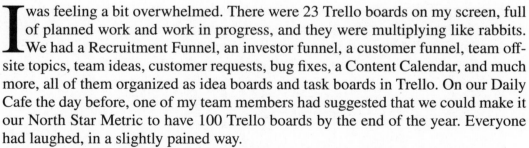

I was feeling a bit overwhelmed. There were 23 Trello boards on my screen, full of planned work and work in progress, and they were multiplying like rabbits. We had a Recruitment Funnel, an investor funnel, a customer funnel, team off-site topics, team ideas, customer requests, bug fixes, a Content Calendar, and much more, all of them organized as idea boards and task boards in Trello. On our Daily Cafe the day before, one of my team members had suggested that we could make it our North Star Metric to have 100 Trello boards by the end of the year. Everyone had laughed, in a slightly pained way.

For your information, Trello is a simple but powerful online tool that helps you manage your work using the concepts of boards, cards, and columns. It is so effective at being both basic and easy to use that people use it for anything, from the collection of baby gifts to the planning of funerals. Trello satisfies the principle of *visualizing your work*. You can better *manage* what you do if you can *see* what you do.

I opened the Feature Ideas board (one of several that we had) and saw dozens of story cards across many columns. I thought to myself how amazing it was that we put so much work into a product and then still did not have something that worked well. I didn't even use our product myself, so I could hardly blame our customers. We were clearly only at the beginning of our Product/Market Fit search. The Trello boards were full of work to do.

I closed the Feature Ideas board on Trello and then clicked the plus icon to create a new one. I gave it the name Book Project. Yes, I had caved in under the pressure (or charms) of my publisher and had decided to write another book. It would be a book about running a startup as an entrepreneur or intrapreneur, hoping to turn it into a scaleup, and trying not to screw up along the way.

The best way to learn something is to write about it. As a startup founder, I had realized that I still had much to learn and had decided to do some field research. With my travels across Europe as a public speaker, it would be easy for me to get interviews with people working at other startups and scaleups, so I could ask them how they managed not to screw things up. I would then capture the learnings in my book and apply them to my own business. It was a brilliant idea. I added the card "Celebrate start of new project" to the first column and closed the board. Now, I was looking at 24 Trello boards. We were one step closer to my team's self-adopted target of 100 boards.

The Kanban Board (see Figure 8.1) might be one of the most important innovations in the world of work. Inspired by signal boards (called *kanban* or 看板 in Japanese) at Toyota, a Kanban Board is a simple two-dimensional board, divided into vertical columns, where every column represents a status within a workflow or value stream. The simplest work statuses would be *planned*, *doing*, and *done*, but you would probably need more columns in between to make the board meaningful. A Kanban Board shows work items moving from left to right, across the various stages of a process, and in doing so, it visualizes the work.

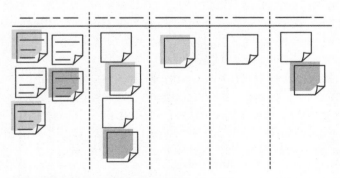

FIGURE 8.1 Kanban Board

The orthodox and militants in the Kanban community will demand that I point out that Trello is not a proper Kanban tool because it supports only one important principle: *visualizing the work*. At the risk of eternal damnation, I say to that, "Bollocks with a herring on top." If Trello does not pass the test then neither does a whiteboard. Each physical and digital tool comes with its own possibilities and constraints. It's up to us to use them in such a way that the result is a proper Kanban Board. You can do that with whiteboards, with Trello boards, and with many other more advanced tools.

The progressives and enlightened in the Kanban community will gently point out to me that a column-based implementation is only *one kind* of a kanban system. And to that, I say, "Kudos with a chocolate on top." Granted, the column-based flow is the most popular visualization, and the one that I focus on in this chapter, but *any* kind of visualization of work, no matter if the work flows upward, downward, sideways, or in circles, can become a kanban system.

Toyota popularized the use of kanban systems as a scheduling and inventory-control technique to achieve just-in-time delivery of car parts through improved collaboration and continuous improvement. But the same principles apply to many kinds of physical or virtual work, including features for a product, content items for a blog, Lean Experiments for a business model, and even chapters for a book. The purpose of a kanban system is to serve as a focal point for a team. It acts as a workflow visualization technique, constantly reminding a team to optimize the flow of the work and helping them to easily see which work items are blocked, are at risk, or need immediate attention for other reasons.

On a standard, column-based Kanban Board, the cards typically represent individual work items. These items arrive in the first column by being moved from a Product Backlog, or some other wish list of ideas, during a planning session with the team. In simple implementations, it is often the first column that represents the wish list of work and the other columns then make up the actual flow of the work in progress.

The columns on a Kanban Board represent the different stages or statuses within the value stream. Apart from the typical planned, doing, and done statuses, other statuses could be *unplanned*, *ready*, *coding*, *testing*, *approval*, *beta*, *live*, and many, many more. These statuses depend on the kind of work item types that you are visualizing. The flow on a Content Kanban will look quite different from the flow designed to manage Lean Experiments. But they are all worth visualizing so that it's easier to manage the work.

The real power of Kanban Boards only becomes apparent when you follow another principle: *limiting the work in progress*. For some types of work, and some statuses within workflows, it makes sense to keep the number of items as small as possible. For example, it doesn't make much sense to be working on 16 product features simultaneously, unless you are the Suleman octuplets. Most likely, your team members shouldn't be working on more than two features at a time, maybe even just one. Therefore, it makes sense to set a Work in Progress (WIP) Limit of just one or two on your *in progress* column. When you have multiple team members working on product features at the same time, you could set the WIP Limit to the maximum number of items that you want the whole team to have in progress at any moment.

The laws of queueing theory indicate that, the smaller you can make the Work in Progress Limits, the faster the work will flow across the Kanban Board. Of course, faster is not always better. What you must strive for is a balance between the work you have in progress and the time it takes to finish it.

It is common practice to write the WIP Limits in the headers of the columns. With a WIP Limit in place on a column, when the maximum number of items is reached, your team members will only allow themselves to move a new card from the previous column into the current one, and start working on it, after another work item is completed in that column, and has moved to the next one. For this reason, it is said that the team works from right-to-left. They focus on completing items on the right first, and they pull new items from the left when there is available capacity on the right. WIP Limits enforce team discipline and a relentless focus on the flow of work.

The cards on Kanban Boards can carry all kinds of signals. During various company visits, I saw boards that had tiny photos of team members who were task owners of the cards. Different colors of stickies are sometimes used to distinguish between different kinds of work, such as new features versus bug fixes or change requests. Some teams play with the orientation of the sticky notes (upright/straight or tilted/queer), and they add stick-

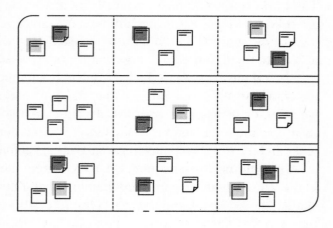

ers, dots, codes, or other annotations. Even the horizontal lanes could be painted gold, silver, and bronze. All this can be done to indicate additional information concerning the work items, such as feature themes, priorities, number of days waiting, number of days in progress, blockers/impediments, and specific stakeholders or Lean Personas.

The experts say that teams should self-organize around their Kanban Board and that they have a joint responsibility for keeping it updated. During their various meetings, a team should *swarm* around their board and discuss the work items to complete first, the items that need attention or unblocking, and the items that should be pulled from columns on the left into available slots on the right, while keeping in mind the WIP Limits in the various stages on the board. The board should signal to relevant parties the items to pick up or hand over to others. To get an even better sense of flow, the team could update a Burn Chart or Cumulative Flow Diagram of their Kanban Board on a regular basis (see Chapter 14).

Experienced teams will try to keep an eye on the number of work items finished per week (*throughput*), the average time it takes for work items to move across the board (*lead time*), and the amount of value-adding work versus the amount of time that work items were just waiting in queues (*flow efficiency*). Such metrics are easiest to obtain when processes have a chance to stabilize over time. This is rather unlikely when your daily business is more accurately described as a colorful and crazy creative chaos, which seems to be the norm among startups. Asking startups to measure their flow efficiency sounds like asking children to stabilize their daily steps, calories, heart rate, and sleep cycles. I feel that young businesses up to and including the Validation (4) stage will benefit from basic Kanban Boards but the advanced stuff will likely have to wait until the Stabilization (5) stage. Allow kids to be kids until they are teenagers. Then they must learn to grow up.

My good friend Jim Benson, co-author of the book *Personal Kanban*, mentions two rules for any kanban system: The first is *Visualize the Work* and the second is *Limit the Work in Progress*. We've seen how you can apply these two principles with Kanban Boards. However, my interviews with various startups and scaleups across Europe have led me to believe that we could add a third principle: *Reduce the Dependencies*. When a work item cannot move forward in your value stream because the work depends on something else, possibly outside the team, you might want to use a big, red sticker to signal a big, bad dependency. Of all the signals that you can add to Kanban Boards, dependencies could be the most important.

For the book that I had promised to write, I decided to contact dozens of startups and scaleups across Europe. One of them was Onefootball in Berlin, where I spoke with Holger Hammel, VP of software engineering. He was one of the people who made me aware of the importance of dependencies.

We have a news team, a scores team, and a platform team. The platform team covers the internal tools; the news team works with the journalists and video people, and the scores team handles statistical data and push notifications. Our company had a big change from component-based teams to cross-functional teams with Android, iOS, DevOps, QA, backend, and frontend all in each team. Previously, component-based teams were continuously blocked. For any feature that we wanted to release, we had work items for iOS, for Android, and probably for the web and the back-end, as well. So for every little feature, we had four or five hand-offs between teams. But now, each cross-functional team handles its own workflow. We have much fewer dependencies than before.

Holger Hammel, VP of software engineering at Onefootball,
Berlin, Germany

Sergei Anikin, CTO of Pipedrive in Tallinn, Estonia, told me a similar story, while showing me around their great-looking offices, full of pipes, tubes, and round, organic forms.

You should have a continuous delivery process where you can deploy as many times per day as you want. This forces you to remove the dependencies between teams and this is what actually speeds up development because teams don't need to wait for others. I believe that most teams probably spend something like—I don't know—50 percent of their time actually doing something useful and the other 50 percent of their time just waiting for somebody else to finish their tasks, or for something else to happen so that they can move on. This is where I have spent a lot of my energy lately: removing all these wait times.

Sergei Anikin, CTO of Pipedrive, Tallinn, Estonia

My chat with Sergei, in Tallinn, Estonia, was the 27th of 30 company interviews. Obviously, I had them all on a new Trello Board called Book Interviews. It was board number 25, my lucky number, and 25 percent toward our target.

For related notes, articles, books, examples, and downloads, check out this web page: https://startup-scaleup-screwup.com/kanban-boards.

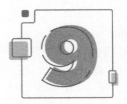

The Invention of Everything Else

Discover the Innovation Vortex, which emerged by combining the Design Thinking approach with the Lean Startup method.

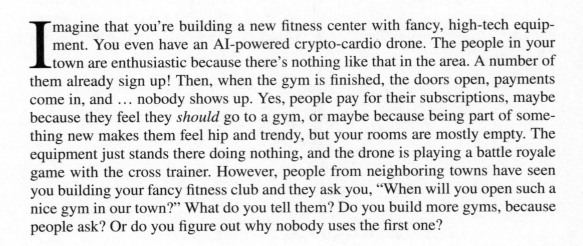

Imagine that you're building a new fitness center with fancy, high-tech equipment. You even have an AI-powered crypto-cardio drone. The people in your town are enthusiastic because there's nothing like that in the area. A number of them already sign up! Then, when the gym is finished, the doors open, payments come in, and … nobody shows up. Yes, people pay for their subscriptions, maybe because they feel they *should* go to a gym, or maybe because being part of something new makes them feel hip and trendy, but your rooms are mostly empty. The equipment just stands there doing nothing, and the drone is playing a battle royale game with the cross trainer. However, people from neighboring towns have seen you building your fancy fitness club and they ask you, "When will you open such a nice gym in our town?" What do you tell them? Do you build more gyms, because people ask? Or do you figure out why nobody uses the first one?

This is the metaphor I always use when people ask us, "When will we get the iOS version?" They've asked us many times because, in the Validation stage, we experiment on the Android platform only. But why would we copy something that doesn't work to another platform? And so, we had many discussions about our Lean Personas, Alberto the External Consultant, and Patricia the Internal Coach, to understand what could make them use the product. We did dozens of customer interviews and ran hundreds of Lean Experiments. We even briefly tried an enterprise offer and then quickly gave up on it. We learned that corporate memberships for the gym just means extra work for the team, while corporations are unlikely to make anyone more eager to play with the AI-powered crypto-cardio drone.

The number one reason for business screwups is the lack of a market need for a new product. In addition to that, user-unfriendly products, unpractical products, and products that are simply unclear and confusing, also contribute to the large number of startup failures. Our team was probably guilty of a bit of everything. If innovation was easy, everyone would be doing it. It all starts with understanding, "Why would a customer show up?"

Empathizing with users, and creating things that work for them, is the realm of Design Thinking. Design Thinking is a human-centered approach for product and service design that matches people's needs with what is technologically feasible and desirable in an attempt to improve their quality of life. By empathizing with the user, and fully understanding the problems and shortcomings of current solutions, design thinkers are sometimes able to achieve breakthrough innovations. The universe sucks because no design thinker was involved creating it.

There are different flavors of Design Thinking, with the two most popular models described as the *Empathize–Define–Ideate–Prototype–Test* loop (promoted by the d.school at Stanford University, see Figure 9.1) and the *Discover–Define–Develop–Deliver* "double diamond" (created by the Design Council in the UK; see Figure 9.2).

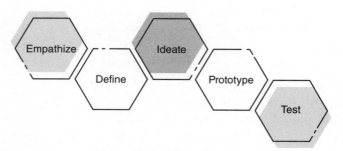

FIGURE 9.1 Design Thinking by the d.school

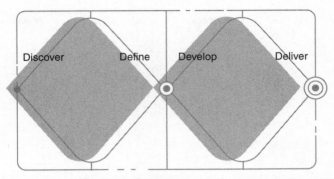

FIGURE 9.2   Design Thinking by the Design Council

What I find particularly interesting about Design Thinking is that the starting point of its approach is feelings rather than facts. Unlike scientists, who have a strong preference for hard evidence and factual data, design thinkers first aim to explore the emotional state of their subjects. When a user says she feels frustrated, a design thinker accepts this as given and will try to understand why before attempting to resolve the frustration by discovering and developing a solution, no matter whether the facts show that the user's frustration is unfounded or justified. Feelings precede facts and design thinkers can discover facts that explain a person's feelings, but the facts won't change those feelings. These statements might make some of my readers squirm and reply that, for innovative product development, we need facts as much as feelings. And I would agree.

Fortunately, the Lean Startup method offers us a chance to balance feelings with facts. The Lean Startup, popularized by Eric Ries and based on the work by Steve Blank, is a popular framework for startups and entrepreneurs that describes how to manage new product development, from an initial idea to a validated product, through many *Build–Measure–Learn* loops (Figure 9.3). Its goal is to shorten the time it takes to understand what product and what business model works for customers by doing many assumptions-driven experiments and aiming for validated learning.

What makes Lean Startup stand out, compared to earlier, less structured approaches to startup management, is its reliance on the scientific method. The Lean Startup differs somewhat from Design Thinking in its focus on facts rather than feelings and emphasizing the use of hypotheses to drive down risks. However, one critical comment about the Lean Startup is that, in the Build–Measure–Learn loop, ideas and hypotheses drop out of nowhere. Sure, there is Steve Blank's strong

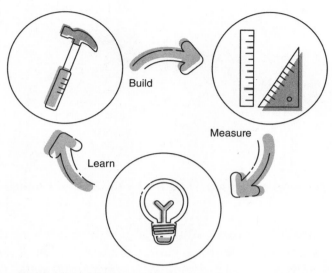

FIGURE 9.3 **The Lean Startup**

recommendation to Get Out of the Building, but the Lean Startup remains vague about any steps between leaving the building and formulating hypotheses. It would be nice if the ideas being rigorously tested in the Lean Startup were based on some empathically obtained insights about customer needs. Another critical comment is that most people are bad at defining and validating hypotheses and just allow their confirmation bias to set their agenda. We will return to that when we discuss Lean Experiments (in Chapter 10).

We can easily address the minor issues with Design Thinking and the Lean Startup by simply overlaying the two approaches, because the strength of the former seems to be the weakness of the latter, and vice versa. Design Thinking specializes in discovering the needs of customers by empathizing with them, understanding their frustrations and desires, and generating ideas for better solutions. Lean Startup excels at testing the generated ideas, in the simplest possible ways, and validating that a solution works and solves a problem. The two models have significant overlap in the middle, but Lean Startup misses a few steps at the beginning and Design Thinking takes a shortcut at the end. Why not simply do it all well by morphing them into one model? It's like creating a dumbbell out of two floor lamps. Very innovative.

I call it the Shiftup Innovation Vortex (see Figure 9.4). It consists of seven different streams of work, swirling into each other.

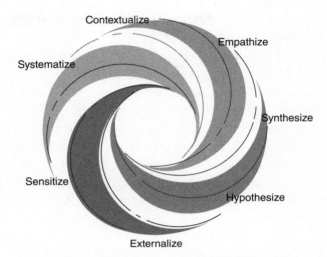

FIGURE 9.4   The Shiftup Innovation Vortex

The first stream of the Innovation Vortex, called **Contextualize**, is about narrowing down innovation to a domain. As much as I hate to say it, you cannot solve all problems in the known universe. You have to focus on something. That means, even before observing people and interviewing them, you need to know *which* people are going to be relevant to you. Before you can start empathizing with your users, you need to decide *who* those users could be. Your Product Vision and your selection of Lean Personas are obviously relevant tools here. The Contextualize stream should lead you to a decision about which part of the universe is worth investigating and improving.

The **Empathize** stream is where the Design Thinking models start and where they shine. This stream is about finding out as much as possible about potential users, their frustrations, aspirations, and experiences. Design thinkers immerse themselves in the environment of their intended users so that they acquire a deeper understanding of all issues through first-hand experience. By empathizing with their users, they aim to set aside their own assumptions and gain true insights into how people experience their situations. Specific techniques used here could be Site Visits, Customer Interviews, Mystery Shopping, Empathy Maps, and perusal of customer data from websites and service desks. The result of this stream is a large pile of unstructured research findings with both emotional and factual content.

In Lean Startup terminology, the work in this stream is often referred to as Get Out of the Building. Despite a lighter emphasis on empathy than in Design Thinking, founders and business leaders of lean startups are definitely advised to immerse themselves in the environments of their intended customers to gain a personal, first-hand understanding of needs and desires, before locking themselves into a specific solution. Some founders even go so far that they volunteer for a while, doing the jobs their customers are doing, or assuming an apprentice or internship role with some of their clients, to learn everything they can about the work, the challenges, the available solutions, and their shortcomings.

Matthäus Schlosser is a product owner at Takeaway.com logistics. In their new offices in Amsterdam, overlooking the former bay water known as the IJ, he told me all about understanding customers.

> *I'm a car driver. I love cars. So the first thing I said to my team was, "Guys, get in my car." We took a box. We took a T-shirt, and we delivered. We delivered for two days and we asked restaurant owners, "Are you happy with our service? How can we improve? What do you like?" And we asked their customers, "Why are you ordering with us? How long did you wait? Did you think the waiting time was okay?" And all kinds of other questions. Obviously, at the end such days, we had a big list of things we wanted to make better, that we needed to improve. Then we did the same through our call center and disposition teams. We would sit down together with them and dispatched orders to our drivers and just answer phone calls from restaurants and from our drivers. We had conversations such as, "Oh, this is too far for you. Why is this too far?" And then the driver said, "Because with the traffic and all, it will take half an hour to get there. It just doesn't make sense for me to drive with a car through the whole city center. Don't you have a bike driver nearby?" And on and on it went.*
>
> *Matthäus Schlosser, product owner at Takeaway.com, Amsterdam,*
> *The Netherlands*

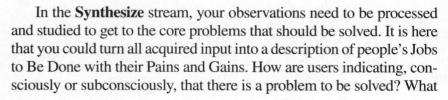

In the **Synthesize** stream, your observations need to be processed and studied to get to the core problems that should be solved. It is here that you could turn all acquired input into a description of people's Jobs to Be Done with their Pains and Gains. How are users indicating, consciously or subconsciously, that there is a problem to be solved? What is it about current products and solutions that is not working for them? The problems that you uncover might confirm what you had identified in the Contextualize stream, but with all the new insights you acquired, you may have changed your mind. The result of this stream should be a clear problem definition in human-centered language.

Based on what you've learned about people's feelings and frustrations, their Jobs to Be Done, and the Pains and Gains to be addressed, you can now start working on ideas for solutions in the **Hypothesize** stream. Generating hypotheses for possible solutions can involve dozens of Design  Thinking techniques, such as Brainstorm, Brainwrite, and Worst Possible Idea. (Use your favorite search engine to learn more about these and other Design Thinking tools.) What are the most radical ways to address your user's frustrations? What are the most original alternative paths to a solution? With your team, you want to get as many ideas as possible so that you can narrow them down to the best candidates for prototyping and testing in the next streams.

An important aspect of Design Thinking, which is not often specifically discussed in Lean Startup, is the possibility of addressing a customer's unarticulated needs. Just by observing people in their environments, it is sometimes possible to see problems that they themselves are not even aware of. They don't know a problem exists until a designer with an external perspective finds unmet needs and devises a solution for them. But coming up with potential solutions to unarticulated needs can only happen when those needs were identified through empathy. The result of trying to meet your customer's articulated and unarticulated needs could be an overview of benefits expressed with a Value Proposition Wheel.

After Sebastien Phlix, senior product manager, and Miloš Lalić, director of product, had shown me around the colorful offices of Typeform in Barcelona, Spain, we sat down to have a quick chat about how design happens at their company, while I was sipping the homemade ginger ale that I was offered at the company's *barception*.

> *It starts with a hypothesis that's shared by all the different functions of the team and that's described as the intended outcome. And then we do lots of things—design sprints, light prototypes using a variety of tools to validate it as early as possible. And the designers, obviously, are heavily involved. It's not like something that only product management does. Design is the whole team.*
> *Sebastien Phlix, senior product manager, and Miloš Lalić, director of product at Typeform, Barcelona, Spain*

What they told me at Typeform was something I heard several times in other conversations with the successful startups and scaleups that I visited and interviewed around Europe. The goal of design is not to define a deliverable or a set of features. It is to affect customer behaviors and make something better. It is about having an impact. So that's what you're after in this stream: generating hypotheses about how to achieve certain outcomes, and your whole team should be involved.

In the **Externalize** stream, your team will be creating something, and making it available to customers, by running Lean Experiments. What you create should be the smallest possible thing that can validate whether you're going in the right direction with your solution. The implementation should be an inexpensive, scaled down, and fast-to-make prototype of the real thing.  In Lean Startup terms, this is called a Minimum Viable Product (MVP). This MVP must be treated as an experiment and the goal is validated learning.

Design thinkers normally use the term *prototype* but, practically, they mean the same thing. MVPs are a specific kind of prototype in the sense that they are meant to test the various hypotheses from the Hypothesize stream by getting customers to interact with the prototypes, and then seeing what happens. The prototypes usually start as low-fidelity MVPs that are used to better understand the problem and solution space, to check how important the problems are for users, and to understand what type of solution would be the best approach. Low-fidelity prototypes can be as simple as online videos or landing pages that test whether customers want to buy into your value proposition. You typically make this kind of prototype in the Expedition stage (2) and Formation stage (3) of the Business Lifecycle to validate Problem-Solution Fit.

Over time, low-fidelity MVPs can evolve into high-fidelity MVPs that are used to match a product that's in development with innovators and early adopters willing to try them, to test product value, pricing, marketing strategy, and communication channels, and to validate hypotheses around user activation, retention, and growth marketing approaches. High-fidelity prototypes can remain MVPs for as long as there is no Product/Market Fit and you are still in the Validation stage (4) of the Business Lifecycle.

The **Sensitize** stream is the sixth stream in the Innovation Vortex. After you have offered one or more prototypes to the user, you must gather data about their effectiveness. You must set up your systems in such a way that your team becomes sensitive to whatever the users are doing. You can think of user interviews, user monitoring, user analytics, and many Growth Hacking

techniques. The focus here is on selecting the most workable, feasible, and effective idea from the various prototypes that you have.

The **Systematize** stream is about deciding what to do with what you've learned. After closely observing people using your prototypes, you should have enough information to see how the results fit into the bigger picture. Did the solution work as intended? Are further improvements necessary? With what you know now, can you decide where in the Innovation  Vortex your attention should go next? Maybe your attention will go back to the beginning, to more contextualizing and empathizing, because the Innovation Vortex is supposed to be an iterative model. Or maybe you have enough data to conduct a Pivot, Patch, or Persevere Meeting with your team and draw some important conclusions about your business model (to be discussed next).

My friends at Typeform continued our conversation about design by telling me how they once screwed up (and then recovered) with a non-iterative approach to their innovation efforts.

> *We had a big redesign project, which wasn't as iterative as it should have been. There were many things that were right about the initial vision and the direction we wanted to go, but then we didn't execute it in an iterative fashion. There were too many things we wanted to achieve simultaneously, which seemed efficient at the time, but that didn't work out as we expected. There were many handoffs and releases arriving way too late, and then we noticed, "Oh no, this actually doesn't work at all." At some point, almost the entire company was working on this redesign project, and it literally took us two years. It was the opposite of how we actually want to do things. Now we see that some of the design decisions, had we iterated, could have been a lot better. We shouldn't have tried to fix everything at once. We could have just focused on the most pressing problems, fix those, iterate, and repeat. But still, the original ideas were really good. We just let ourselves be drawn into this non-iterative approach to innovation that seemed efficient when we started but that cost us a lot of effort to get out of.*
>
> *Sebastien Phlix, senior product manager, and Miloš Lalić, director of product at Typeform, Barcelona, Spain*

Both Design Thinking and the Lean Startup insist on iterative approaches to innovation, and neither suggests that their steps always need to be performed in a linear manner. You can do work in any step at any time. The focus of design thinkers is a bit more on empathizing with users, while the focus of lean startuppers is somewhat more on the validation of hypotheses. For real innovation, all steps are relevant. The different steps are best understood as different operating modes for your team. It is true that they commonly follow each other, but backtracking and hop-skip-jumping across the seven steps is fine. That's why I prefer to visualize the innovation process as a vortex of streams rather than a sequence of steps.

I didn't invent the vortex. I merely discovered it by merging the Design Thinking and Lean Startup methods. Work happens in all streams; they all swirl together, and in the middle, you find innovation, peace, quiet, and a cup of chai with a piece of lemon meringue pie.

If you aim for true innovation, and you hope to show off an amazing product to customers in a demo, or to investors in a Pitch Deck, your team needs to work across all streams of the Shiftup Innovation Vortex.

For related notes, articles, books, examples, and downloads, check out this web page: https://startup-scaleup-screwup.com/innovation-vortex.

The Terminal Experiment

Validate hypotheses with Lean Experiments so that you can Pivot, Patch, or Persevere on your way to Business/Market Fit.

We had been working for more than half a year and our team had still not achieved Product/Market Fit. It made me feel anxious. How much longer would it take until we had a viable business? Why doesn't our kid grow up faster?

As a founder, entrepreneur, or intrapreneur, to get to Product/Market Fit, and then Business/Market Fit, you turn your vision of a business into hypotheses for each piece of your Business Quilt and then you start experimenting and validating. This exploration is your main focus in the Validation (4) and Stabilization (5) stages of the Business Lifecycle. Do you have the right audience? Do you have the right idea for a solution? Does the product offer the right benefits? Does the product relieve a Pain or add a Gain? Are people using it? Does the revenue model show signs that it's working? It can take many iterations, and many interactions with potential customers, to get positive answers to those questions.

Founders often think that getting funded and hiring a team are their biggest challenges. They're wrong. Almost everyone underestimates the time and effort it takes to validate their business model. Several sources indicate that the primary reason for failure of startups is a business model that doesn't work.

Your number one challenge is not the money and it's not your team. They are number two and number three, respectively. Number one is your business. Proper funding and a good team won't help you when you fail to achieve Product/Market Fit.

And how long does it normally take to find Product/Market Fit, you asked? Three years, says Marc Wesselink, managing partner at Startupbootcamp.

You need three years to build a company. I often say you need to create a base camp. And for first base it takes three years, and that's a team with product-market fit in some scalable way. My first two companies were successful. But the third, fourth, fifth, sixth, and seventh were failures and the failures were all within three years.
Marc Wesselink, managing partner at Startupbootcamp, Amsterdam, The Netherlands

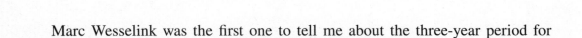

Marc Wesselink was the first one to tell me about the three-year period for Product/Market Fit. In other interviews, the same number came up several times.

We were 9, 10 people about 15 months ago. Now we are at 50. So, you can see our switch to becoming a scaleup. It took us three years and nine months of scrimping, surviving, and the founders taking no salaries during that period. And then, all of a sudden, things just clicked.
Paul Dolman-Darrall, CEO of Gamevy, London, United Kingdom

That was the input from Paul Dolman-Darrall, CEO of Gamevy in London, who led me to believe that a three-year period to get to Product/Market Fit might be an average, not a maximum.

Esther Gons, co-author of *The Corporate Startup* and founder/partner/investor at NEXT Amsterdam joined me over a Zoom call from Amsterdam.

I would say it's a minimum of three years. You need those three years to validate your revenue model, but people underestimate the stage where they start scaling up. In those first three years, you may have validated your business model for the early evangelists. You've proven that they like your product and that they want to pay for it. But at scale, early evangelists are probably not enough. When you start scaling up, you will have to address new customer segments to reach a larger number of customers. And that means you'll have to start all over, validating your business model for a new audience. That could easily take another three years.

Esther Gons, founder/partner/investor at NEXT, Amsterdam,
The Netherlands

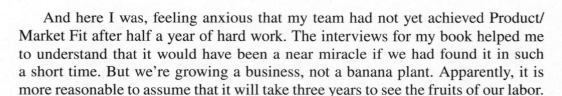

And here I was, feeling anxious that my team had not yet achieved Product/ Market Fit after half a year of hard work. The interviews for my book helped me to understand that it would have been a near miracle if we had found it in such a short time. But we're growing a business, not a banana plant. Apparently, it is more reasonable to assume that it will take three years to see the fruits of our labor.

In a period of roughly three years (less than that would be awesome), you need to make sure that all the pieces of your Business Quilt are in place and properly validated. You do that by endlessly hopping around the Innovation Vortex and by running many Lean Experiments, which you can prepare in four simple steps.

Step 1 is to **Identify Assumptions**. You must describe the things that you want to be true for your business to succeed. These are sometimes called leap-of-faith assumptions. This could be your idea about the size of the market, the willingness of your customers to change behaviors, the availability of technologies for building your product, and so on. It's best to use the various pieces of your Business Quilt for categorizing those assumptions. You will have many! Place the riskiest assumptions at the top so you can deal with them first.

Step 2 is to **Define Hypotheses**. You need to formulate your assumptions in such a way that they become testable with a clear hypothesis statement. As the scientists say, make your assumption falsifiable and see if you can prove yourself wrong. Without an idea of what you want to happen, you cannot evaluate success or failure. And you don't learn if you can't fail.

Step 3 is to **Define Metrics**. If you can't measure it, you can't manage it. So, make sure that you can measure whether your hypotheses are proven false. By making things measurable, you switch from subjective and political conversations to evidence-based decision-making on your team.

Step 4 is to **Identify Experiments**. You now need to agree on the actions you will take to test your hypotheses and measure the results. Try to make it the smallest possible experiment that gives you the quickest, most reliable answer. And make sure to contain the risk of failure. The worst thing that can happen when your experiment fails must be something that you are still able to handle.

Notice that the best experiments are those where you try to prove yourself *wrong*, like a good scientist tries to do. It is always easy to prove yourself right and many entrepreneurs and intrapreneurs allow confirmation bias to take over and pick and choose the data that neatly matches their convictions, which leads to a false sense of security. See if you can prove yourself wrong.

When you define a hypothesis statement, you might want to consider a format like this one:

We believe [*this assumption is true*]. We will know we're wrong when we [*specific repeatable action*] and as a result get [*qualitative and/or quantitative feedback*].

For example:

"We believe *customers are willing to pay EUR 19 per month*. We will know we're wrong when *we direct 100 free users to a paywall* and as a result get *only 20% or less conversion*."

Defining Lean Experiments is part of the work that you do on the Hypothesize stream in the Innovation Vortex. On the other streams, you work to make the experiments available, measure the activity, and then discuss the results. Were your assumptions proven false? Do you need other metrics or more experiments? Do you have enough confidence that you were right? By thinking like a scientist, your unit of progress becomes what we call validated learning. As a founder and entrepreneur, your aim is to learn as much as possible in the shortest amount of time.

Lean Experiments should be quick and simple. They usually lack the rigor to call them true scientific tests, but that's okay. The goal is to get enough confidence that your business model seems to be working. You can add Lean Experiments to a Kanban Board so that your team can keep track of the ones in progress.

Many founders see the iterative development of Minimum Viable Products as the main approach to seeking Product/Market Fit. A low-fidelity MVP may start out as a simple video or landing page that validates whether customers are willing to sign up for a solution (that doesn't exist yet). In subsequent iterations, the MVP could turn into a series of throwaway prototypes. Ultimately, it could become a high-fidelity MVP, a simplistic but working version of the real product. Each time a new version of an MVP is delivered to (usually a small set of) customers, it wraps one or more Lean Experiments, and from the response of those customers to the MVPs, the business should be able to do some significant validated learning.

What founders sometimes forget is that the Minimum Viable Product is usually about … (drumroll) … the *product*. It often has little to do with other parts of the business model, such as the Channels, the Revenues, the Customer Relationships, or other pieces of the Business Quilt. But you need to validate hypotheses in all these areas. In fact, for some businesses, the product itself might be the easiest part. When it comes to creating Lean Experiments, the relevant question is always, what is the most important thing to learn now? That most important thing will not always require the release of a new MVP.

As a final word about Lean Experiments, it is important to understand that one experiment is often not enough to validate (or invalidate) a hypothesis. For many assumptions, you need to run multiple tests, and you need to be systematic about how to perform them. It's like looking at a problem from multiple angles. One single view may not be enough to draw a conclusion.

With the results from your experiments coming in all the time, you need to discuss regularly whether you're making good progress testing your assumptions and validating your entire business model. It's important to have a regular Strategy Meeting where you review the status of your Business Quilt and Lean Experiments and decide whether any major changes to your strategy are needed. You should ask yourself all the time, "Do we have evidence that our current strategy is getting us closer to our vision? Should we pivot, patch, or persevere?"

The term *Pivot* is used for a structural course correction of your business. A pivot is a change in strategy without a change in vision. Pivoting is what you should consider when you conclude that you're not making any progress (or not enough) toward Product/Market Fit in the Validation stage, and Business/Market Fit in the Stabilization stage. It means replacing everything in one or more of the pieces of your Business Quilt with a different set of assumptions. This could be a different problem statement, different customer segments, a different revenue model, or even an entirely different solution.

You can define a pivot as the realization that your business model is not working and that you need to replace one or more of its components. If you're not completely changing any pieces that make up your business model, you're not really pivoting. Note that a pivot does not mean starting from scratch. You completely replace *some* of the pieces, but not *all* of them. It's not uncommon for startups to experience a handful of pivots during the Formation (3) and Validation (4) stages of their lifecycle. Two common reasons for screwups among young businesses are a pivot not done in time, and a pivot executed badly.

I want to introduce the term *Patch* for a smaller change to some of the pieces of your Business Quilt. You're not wiping any of the pieces clean, but you replace a number of individual assumptions in them. What you have seems not to be working well enough. This could be about a different pricing model (while you keep the revenue model the same), different priorities of customer segments (while the collection of segments remains unchanged), or a significant change to the product features (while not really changing any of its benefits). If you do your job well as a business leader, such patches to your business model should happen quite frequently. Part of the strategy works, but another part doesn't. You replace the bad parts without losing the good parts.

The term *Persevere* is used to indicate that you simply move forward with the planned business model. You validate more assumptions and build more and more confidence that things are working as you hoped they

would. Persevering with your current business strategy means
that you keep believing in what you set out to achieve, and you
implement small changes and updates every day to make progress toward your goals. Every day, you have new ideas for
building your product, new measurements to check, and
new opportunities for learning. By validating more and
more assumptions, you move the business model closer
and closer to Product/Market Fit and Business/Market
Fit. Examples of persevering are understanding which
features are used by customers and which ones are
not, learning which texts, colors, and styles generate
the best response rates in e-mail campaigns, and figuring out how to most effectively convert free users to paid plans.

Pivoting, patching, and persevering for a business are like migrating, upgrading, and living for a person. Migrating to another place (pivoting) is something
most of us do only rarely. Upgrading our homes (patching) with a new floor, a
redesigned kitchen, or better Wi-Fi is something that happens more frequently.
Enjoying our daily lives (persevering) is what we hope to do every day.

 And how do you know when you finally found Product/Market Fit, you ask?
You'll know.

Some experts say that you've found Product/Market Fit when "eager customers are ripping the product out of your hands" and when "you have difficulty
keeping up with demand." Others say you found it when "your product grows
exponentially with no marketing, just by word of mouth" and when "investors are
banging on your door for the privilege of investing in your business." It all sounds
convincing but such statements cover only part of the truth. I learned that a little
bit more is needed.

When you evaluate your Business Quilt, you must understand that Product/
Market Fit is a subset of Business/Market Fit. And Business/Market Fit requires
validating *at least* all your hypotheses for Problem, Solution, Customer Segments,
Unique Value Proposition, Channels, Revenue Streams, and Cost Structure. And
probably one or two more, depending on your business. The quotes mentioned
previously in this chapter merely seem to cover Problem, Solution, and Unique

Value Proposition. When people are enthusiastically crawling all over your business, it doesn't mean that you found a big market or a sustainable revenue model, for example. So that won't be enough. All relevant pieces need to be in place, and validated, *before* you can start scaling things up.

One of the most common ways that startups fail is scaling prematurely. The idea that a startup is ready for prime time when customers and investors are all throwing money at it is a dangerous one. Product/Market Fit is not Business/Market Fit. It is tempting for entrepreneurs to scale things up as soon as the funds pour in and to then spend all that money on growth. When they haven't properly validated the other pieces of the business model, there is a good chance that things will go wrong.

In our line of business, we have one magic word: Product/Market Fit. Build a product that fits a market. Many companies hire 25 or 30 people because they think they have Product/Market Fit, but it's total bullshit. And then they scale too early. They fall in love with their own solution, but they have not created a product for a problem in a specific market segment. In my experience, that's the number one fuckup among startups. I mean screwup. Excuse my language.
Marc Wesselink, managing partner at Startupbootcamp,
Amsterdam, The Netherlands

And with that, I finished my interview with Marc Wesselink, managing partner at Startupbootcamp, leaving him so he could get back to his many startups.

Validating a business model is hard work. But don't worry, you don't have to test everything at the same time. Most likely, the Value Proposition, Customer Segments, Solution, Revenue Model, and Cost Structure come first. These pieces are probably the ones you want to focus on in the Validation stage (4) of your Business Lifecycle. Most of your work on the other pieces, such as Channels and Customer Relationships, can wait until Stabilization (5).

Despite the different definitions, what all experts seem to agree on is that Product/Market Fit, followed by Business/Market Fit, is the precondition for scaling up your business. To me, this means that the pieces of your Business

Quilt are validated and fixed without requiring any further pivots or patches. But don't expect things to stay that way. Markets and competitors are always changing. You may need to revisit your validated assumptions sooner rather than later in order to retain the Product/Market Fit that you so valiantly fought to achieve. Don't let the assumption that nothing will ever change turn into an unintended, terminal experiment.

For related notes, articles, books, examples, and downloads, check out this web page: https://startup-scaleup-screwup.com/lean-experiments.

Fables and Reflections

Get together with your team for an Agile Retrospective to do some reflection and work on your Improvement Backlog.

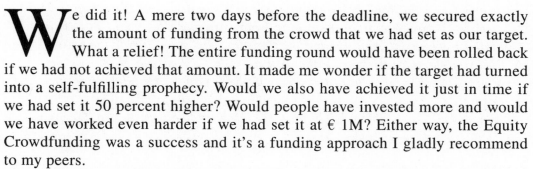

We did it! A mere two days before the deadline, we secured exactly the amount of funding from the crowd that we had set as our target. What a relief! The entire funding round would have been rolled back if we had not achieved that amount. It made me wonder if the target had turned into a self-fulfilling prophecy. Would we also have achieved it just in time if we had set it 50 percent higher? Would people have invested more and would we have worked even harder if we had set it at € 1M? Either way, the Equity Crowdfunding was a success and it's a funding approach I gladly recommend to my peers.

Our successful round of funding called for a moment of reflection with the entire team. I looked at the board full of colorful sticky notes while my teammates were organizing their feedback and improvement suggestions into clusters. The note that read, "Too many meetings" was grouped together with "I can't get things done because of all the meetings." I looked around for another group of notes that

I was expecting. Ah, there it was. The stickies that said, "Not enough communication" and "More collaboration needed" had found each other in another cluster. They want to see each other less and work together more. Less sugar, more cookies. Brilliant. There were other stickies about "Funding stress," "Too many Trello boards," "Make daily cafes more fun," and much more. I added my own improvement note that said, "Try continuous funding next time."

An Agile Retrospective is a team meeting held on a regular basis, often every few weeks, in which team members share feedback and improvement suggestions with each other about their teamwork, the processes they are using, the product they are making, and the environment in which they work. Often conducted with the help of a facilitator, it is a shared moment of reflection on how to become more efficient and effective as a team. In a retrospective, team members share facts and feelings, in a respectful way, about the work they did and any events that happened that had an impact on their performance, without resorting to blame or finger-pointing.

Boris Diebold, CTO at Seven Senders, had invited me for an early Friday morning chat at their offices in Berlin. It was warm that day, so we sat outside on a roof terrace.

Our teams can organize their work however they want. However, at the minimum, I want them to do something like a planning, and I want them to have a regular review or demo with their stakeholders. I also want to see some kind of learning. Whether they do a retrospective every week or every second week or every month, I don't really care. But when I don't see any action items emerging from retrospectives then I'm coming in and I get pushy. And again, how they do their retros inside the team, for example, with stickies on the wall or with a TV screen, that's not up to me. They organize that themselves. I act as coach and adviser, if they need me.

Boris Diebold, CTO at Seven Senders, Berlin, Germany

The goal of an Agile Retrospective is to have a team take ownership of the issues they are facing and to take responsibility for solving any problems and improving their work. A regular cadence of peer-to-peer feedback enables them to adopt a culture of continuous improvement. For many self-organizing teams, such an exercise can feel very empowering and motivating. For some teams, however, it feels like a waste of their time. In case of the latter, this problem can be addressed by first asking them if they are mindless drones or smart professionals, and then organizing an Agile Retrospective to fix their Agile Retrospectives. It would help if they had a good outside facilitator.

As much as possible, all members of a team should participate in a team's retros. In larger companies, it is common practice not to invite managers because their presence during the peer-to-peer reflection might inhibit the free flow of opinions. Managers could be an obstacle to an honest discussion of performance issues because some people tend to shut down when their managers are present, despite everyone's best intentions. This is much less of an issue with small startup teams, but it does mean that I don't feel guilty when I occasionally miss our team retros. I want our team to feel free to discuss the root causes of problems, and sometimes that root cause might be me.

Agile Retrospectives can be organized in eight steps. In the **Open** step, your team may find it helpful to have a small ritual. Similar to dinner rituals, exercise rituals, and sleep rituals, it can be good to have a standard way to begin (and end) the team's retros because this helps participants to get into the right mood and adopt the right mindset for this important meeting.

For example, the team can introduce a check-in protocol where each person confirms their presence and their commitment to support trust and transparency during the session. You want everyone in the group to feel heard and understood and you want people to share their concerns without blame or retribution. They could print a poster with the team's retrospective rules on which everyone signs their names, or they could ask each person explicitly to honor the team's code of conduct. Some teams simply read the Prime Directive as offered in the book *Project Retrospectives* by Norman L. Kerth:

"Regardless of what we discover, we understand and truly believe that everyone did the best job he or she could, given what was known at the time, his or her skills and abilities, the resources available, and the situation at hand."

The implementation doesn't matter much. What matters is that they start (and finish) their retros with certain behavioral triggers to get everyone in the proper state of mind.

In the **Reflect** step of a retrospective, your team starts by looking at their Improvement Board (if they have one). The Improvement Board is an optional simple Kanban Board that shows the improvement items that were prioritized in previous retros. They follow up on these items to see if any progress was achieved. Hopefully, any impediments and other issues have been properly addressed and resolved. If not, reprioritization may be needed.

In the **Collect** step, the team gathers new input. There are many ways of doing this. Entire books and websites are dedicated to vast overviews of retrospective techniques that, quite miraculously, nearly always involve a whiteboard and sticky notes. Sometimes, they require specific game cards or other materials.

In my opinion, unlike the opening and closing steps of the meeting, this part of the retrospective should *not* be a standard ritual. Some issues only become apparent by looking at them from a specific angle or perspective. If the team follows the same retrospective format each time, the participants are likely to keep reporting the same problems; the meetings might become stale, and, at some point, the practice may even be discarded. But if the team chooses a different technique each time, chances are higher that the sessions remain interesting and engaging, and that the team is able to identify different problems or see the same problems in a different light.

Some of the most popular retrospective techniques ask team members to write answers to a few questions, such as:

1. What went well? + What can be improved?
2. What made us *mad*? + What made us *sad*? + What made us *glad*?
3. What did we *love*? + What did we *loathe*? + What did we *learn*? + What did we *lack*?

In this step, the goal is *divergent thinking*. It is intended to only collect input by asking all participants to write their thoughts on sticky notes and put them on the wall. The issues reported can be about anything: bottlenecks while running Lean Experiments, problems with the Kanban Boards, confusion around the Value Proposition Wheel,

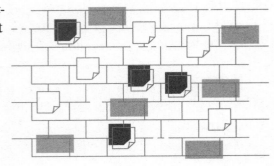

and much more. Brief explanations of reported issues might be useful, but full discussions are not desirable at this point in the meeting and should be held off until the following steps. First, get everything out of people's minds and onto the wall. Let every team member submit their opinions, stories, examples, and fables. The wall should be covered with colorful sticky notes and everyone should understand the meaning of what was written.

The **Organize** step is about the categorization of all input. The team will find that, quite often, the same feedback is shared by different participants. Half the team says there are too many meetings; the other half claims there's not enough collaboration. In this step, the team clusters the input into similar topics and achieves convergence on the insights. The team will do this  grouping as a collaborative exercise until they achieved consensus on all categories. (One would think that, if they can do this easily, they can ditch the notes about collaboration right there.)

The **Celebrate** step is intended to briefly identify the things that went well, that people are happy about, or that are just worth mentioning and that don't require any problem-solving. Preceding the team's moment of critical introspection with things that are already great is a good way of getting them prepared for some deeper soul-searching. Some facilitators report that they place the  celebrate step at the beginning of the retrospective, just after the opening, because it sets a positive tone for the rest of the meeting.

In the **Learn** step, after the feel-good moment, the team matches the other issues that they reported with the items on their Improvement Backlog (if they have one). The Improvement Backlog is the place where they keep all issues that were found during earlier retrospectives. Are some of the issues new?  Did they generate more insights on problems that were already on the list? The focus of this step is to learn and be aware of anything that is important.

At this point, the team should refrain from defining action items and just add their impediments, obstacles, and frustrations to their Improvement Backlog. There is no need to define action items for issues that they have not yet prioritized.

Holger Hammel, VP of software engineering at Onefootball in Berlin, Germany, shared with me his view on team retrospectives.

What we did recently is a nice timeline retrospective to see how, for instance, the recent change in team structure impacted our teams—seeing clusters of things that were good or not so good and that were driving the mood. We had some very good conversations about that, which was quite helpful. We're really focusing on having a good process for learning from incidents. We see there is a system failing there, and then it's failing again, and then it should be like all alarm bells are ringing. It's not about just fixing this one failure. It's about how to learn quickly from all failures. At the last meeting, I was surprised to see how well the conversations were going actually. Everyone was very open. There was no blaming. They had a nice, constructive atmosphere.

Holger Hammel, VP of software engineering at
Onefootball, Berlin, Germany

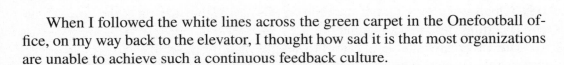

When I followed the white lines across the green carpet in the Onefootball office, on my way back to the elevator, I thought how sad it is that most organizations are unable to achieve such a continuous feedback culture.

In the **Prioritize** step, after your team has updated their Improvement Backlog, it is time for them to discuss what issues to act on until the next retrospective. When some problems emerge again and again during the retro meetings, does that mean their priority should go up? Or is it time for the team to accept that some issues are just a fact of work-life and that they can be removed from the list? The team decides what is worth focusing on, what the desired end state is, and moves those items from the waiting list on the Improvement Backlog to their work in progress on the Improvement Board.

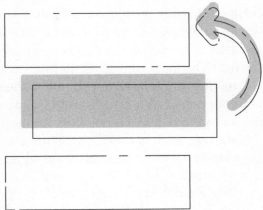

Your team should take care not to take on too much work. It is tempting to try and solve many problems at a time, but experience shows that most teams are not able to do that. They should keep it modest and probably pick not more than two or three issues to solve. It is demotivating to realize in the next retro that (almost) nothing out of 20 planned improvements got done. Therefore, pick just a few, turn those into action items, and get some of the participants to take ownership to see them through to completion.

In the **Close** step, your team can wrap up the retrospective in a fun and inspiring way. Again, they could make it a ritual to indicate that the session is over and that everyone can switch their attention back to getting work done and getting problems solved. For example, with a quick Fist of Five (like my team does at the end of their Daily Cafes), the team members can rate their retrospective for its effectiveness level (how useful was this) and its engagement level (how enjoyable was it).

Agile Retrospectives are facilitated meetings. A facilitator makes sure that all participants are heard and that the rules for optimal collaboration are properly followed. Facilitators can also take care of the logistics of the meetings, find new retro techniques, and pick the tools that best match with what the team needs at the moment. Without a dedicated facilitator, teams run the risk that everyone is too busy to do these meetings properly, or they might even forget about them entirely.

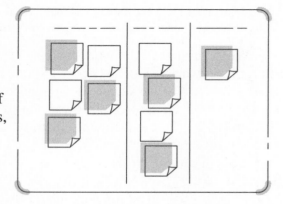

If you don't have the luxury of an outside facilitator, it is perfectly acceptable to have the role inside your team. Maybe your team members can rotate in and out of this role. This might increase curiosity and engagement among the participants because style and preferences for organizing the retros will differ among the facilitators.

Agile Retrospectives are all-hands meetings. They come with a cost in terms of person-hours. So, you better make sure that your team's retros are well prepared and well executed to get the most out of them, or else the practice gets discredited and discarded, and you will throw away a major driver for continuous improvement in your business. If, during certain hectic periods, you feel you cannot afford to organize separate retrospective meetings, then I suggest you cheat and include a few retrospective questions in some of your regular meetings.

That's exactly what Rickard Svedenmark, chief technical officer of Fishbrain, does with his teams in Stockholm, Sweden.

In all my meetings, I always end with the question, "What should we do differently next time?" If you do that in all meetings, every time, you don't need everyone to vote on all kinds of issues. You don't need to be scientific and you don't need to do all those retrospectives. Just ask this one question, take the first answer, and when everybody agrees and says, "Yeah, that might be a good idea," you will get to a very good place very fast.
Rickard Svedenmark, CTO at Fishbrain, Stockholm, Sweden

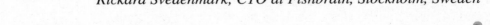

For related notes, articles, books, examples, and downloads, check out this web page: https://startup-scaleup-screwup.com/agile-retrospectives.

Kings of the North

Navigate your business in the right direction using a North Star Metric, with the help of Support Metrics and Check Metrics.

I was not happy.

I came back from a two-week vacation in Japan to find that the team had made almost no progress in the areas that I had prioritized before I left. Instead, they had worked on some other themes of which I didn't see the relevance. I tried to blame myself as much as I did the others. I had not conveyed my objectives well and I didn't understand their explanations. I foresaw another note urging for "better communication" in our next Agile Retrospective.

On top of that, there was no sign of our customers enthusiastically using our product. There was no gamification. No intrinsic motivation. No fun. Fortunately, the money from the Equity Crowdfunding campaign had finally arrived. I had remotely finalized the legal process from my hotel in Tokyo and our cash reserves had been replenished. Thank God! Because of this financial support, we felt a vote of confidence from the crowd that we *could* solve this problem, but also a strong responsibility that we *should*.

And so, we decided to do another patch of our business model. It was not a pivot, because nothing drastic in the business would change. We didn't replace any of the pieces of our Business Quilt. But we also didn't just want to persevere as if nothing was wrong. Our product clearly needed a significant patch. It seemed that an important part was missing on our Value Proposition Wheel. We generated ideas, discussed the options, and initiated some Lean Experiments in a new area. We felt thrilled. We had regained a sense of *focus*.

A lack of focus is yet another top reason for failure among young businesses. If you don't pay all of your attention to the things that matter most, your startup easily becomes a screwup. Your Business Quilt has a Key Metrics piece. This means that you should agree on how to measure achievements as a team. Being a founder, entrepreneur, or intrapreneur, it is crucial that you know exactly what needs to be done, what the next milestone should be, and how you will measure progress. You may have investors watching over your shoulders. Find out what matters most and then measure your progress in that direction!

There are 100 billion stars in the universe. And there are 100 billion wrong things your team could be working on. I think my team knows even more than that. A North Star Metric, sometimes referred to as the One Metric That Matters (OMTM), is a measure that, like its namesake, the Pole Star, helps your team to navigate in the right direction. With so much data all around you, it is easy for your team members to drown in numbers and focus on the wrong ones. They can get distracted trying to optimize short-term growth metrics rather than striving for long-term health. That's why it's useful to have one objective to concentrate on that takes precedence over everything else.

A well-defined North Star Metric enables a cross-functional team to sail together toward a common goal. The objective should be easy to understand for everyone and help the team make decisions when working on things such as Lean Experiments, Product Backlog, Product Roadmap, and Content Calendar.

Rather than measuring the amount of work done, a good North Star Metric gets a team to deliver maximum value for users and customers. For example, our team is currently measuring and optimizing the *Number of Content Items Viewed per Week per Person*, assuming that a happy user will consume more content. This is a crucial aspect of this practice, and often overlooked, so I will repeat it here. The North Star Metric should capture and represent *value to users and customers.* If you focus on a metric that does that, the success of your business is much more likely to follow.

The best metrics depend on your product or service. Don't fall into the trap of copying *vanity metrics* from blog posts and from other companies that are only meant to brag about achievements and stroke people's egos. For example, *Total Users Acquired* is a terrible candidate for a North Star Metric because the size of your user base makes *you* feel great, not your users. *Number of Daily Active Users* is a suspicious candidate because it could nudge your team toward finding more *new* users rather than improving the value for *current* users. And *Monthly Recurring Revenue* is also a bad North Star Metric because no crowd of customers is ever going to say, "Wow, we feel great paying you so much money each month!" Unless you're in the business of starting a new religion.

It's not difficult to test if you have a decent North Star Metric. Does the metric correlate strongly with the actual engagement of your customers with the solution? When the number goes up, is that because people recognize the value the product has for them? Ask yourself if the metric correlates with the number of times your *users* say, "Wow, this product is great!" If, instead, the metric correlates with the number of times your *investors* say, "Wow, this business is great!," you have the wrong north star.

Good North Star Metrics typically fall into either of three categories: (1) the amount of people's *attention* you can capture with your product (think Spotify and Rovio, and for example, *Minutes of Player Activity per Month per User*); (2) the size of the *transactions* you can generate (think Takeaway and Zalando, and for example, *Total Order Size per Customer*); and (3) the amount of *productivity* you can generate for your users (think TransferWise and Taxify, and for example, *Transfers or Rides per Customer per Month*).

It was a lovely sunny day when I arrived at a provider of user experience analytics in Paris. The company surprised me by letting an entire team do the interview with me. Afterward, on my audio recording, it was difficult to identify who had said what during our dynamic discussion, in which they shared some really smart insights.

> *What is important for our customers is how we can decrease the time their users spend on the platform. Our goal is to reduce the effort of finding information, which might be the opposite of what others would think*

intuitively. Many people would say, "I want to increase the time our users spend on the platform." Well, no. We want to decrease that, because if we succeed in decreasing the time users stay on the platform and increase the number of times they are coming on the platform, it means they find more of what they want, but with less effort.

I find it useful to distinguish between *result metrics* and *action metrics*. Result metrics are like the scoreboard for your team. They indicate whether you're winning or losing the game. Action metrics are like the field positions, steps, jumps, passes, and violations during the game. They are the things you do as a team in the hope of driving up the score. Action metrics are fully within your team's *scope of control*. Result metrics are not within your scope of control, but they are within your *scope of influence*. This is why some people talk about input metrics versus output metrics, or leading indicators versus lagging indicators. But I think the simplest distinction is actions versus results (see Figure 12.1).

The best North Star Metrics are results-oriented. They focus on the outcomes of your team and the impact they have on your customers. The problem is that you cannot focus only on result metrics because they are too broad, too far away, and not actionable. It takes time for your actions to turn into results. And by the time you see the results, it might be too late to make any changes. It's true that only the final score is the One Metric That Matters but to get there you'll need to agree on Many Metrics That Move You.

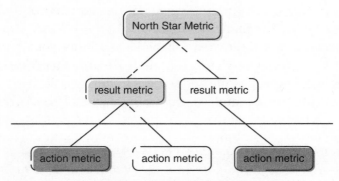

FIGURE 12.1 The North Star Metric with Result Metrics and Action Metrics

To make things even more challenging, results depend on scope. You may have a winning score for the current game but maybe you lose the next one. Multiple small outcomes in the short term are needed for a few bigger outcomes in the long term. Fact is, there are some things you have direct control over now (your actions) and all the rest is just results with various short-term and long-term effects.

Deciding on the scope of your North Star Metric is a decision you have to make with your team. Do you track the value created per week or per month? Do you capture value for one Lean Persona or for several at a time? Do you focus on one area of the Value Proposition Wheel or does the metric cover all parts of the wheel? You have many options for picking the scope and it's no problem to update your North Star Metric regularly over time. In fact, this is certain to happen during the different stages of your Business Lifecycle. Like my team, yours will probably switch north stars several times during Validation (4) because you are exploring. And the focus will certainly change again when you move up to the Acceleration stage (6).

Assuming that you are able to agree on a North Star Metric, you will probably also want to select a few Support Metrics with a smaller scope that show you earlier results in the right direction. After all, it might take some time for your north star to reflect a positive change. Percentage ball possession and the number of goals made in a match are supporting metrics for the final score of the game. For a company such as Zalando, the users' browsing behaviors in the app and the total value of items in their shopping carts are Support Metrics for the North Star Metric of *Total Order Size per Customer*, which only changes after each order.

The purpose of monitoring a few additional metrics that support the North Star is to make changes early when things aren't going as you had hoped. This is exactly what a football coach does when he swaps players during a game based on the current score up to that moment. And if, unlike my team, you paid attention to my ideas about the north star, you will understand that your North Star Metric itself could become a Support Metric for another North Star Metric further away, when you increase your scope to take in a bigger view.

I visited Dublin, Ireland, three days after my trip to Paris. All of Europe was basking in a heat wave and, like many other areas on the continent, Dublin experienced the warmest and driest summer on record. John Collins, director of content at Intercom, talked with me about metrics.

In general, I think we're a little bit skeptical and we don't always just accept common wisdom. Sometimes, in the startup world, there are too

many people looking for easy answers and simple formulas for success. It's the same with the North Star Metric. Is there ever only one metric that's going to guide your whole company? I think different metrics will be important at different times. Maybe your engagement isn't as good as it should be. People aren't using your product as much as you'd like them to. Then, obviously, you focus on those metrics. Maybe your new user growth slows down. Then you need to think about how you're going to fill that funnel of leads who will turn into customers. There's going to be different things at different moments. As humans, we all want to be able to say, "There is just the one thing, and it's easy." But life is messier than that. We shouldn't be too religious about these things.
    John Collins, director of content at Intercom, Dublin, Ireland

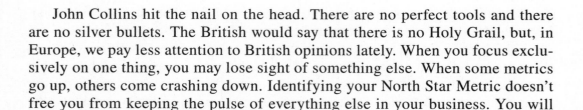

John Collins hit the nail on the head. There are no perfect tools and there are no silver bullets. The British would say that there is no Holy Grail, but, in Europe, we pay less attention to British opinions lately. When you focus exclusively on one thing, you may lose sight of something else. When some metrics go up, others come crashing down. Identifying your North Star Metric doesn't free you from keeping the pulse of everything else in your business. You will probably want to have a few Check Metrics that monitor some of the other important parts.

For example, for a business such as Spotify, optimizing the *Minutes of Music per Month per User* could be important but it doesn't cover the happiness of employees or the profitability of the company. In complex organizations, everything is interrelated, and tradeoffs between metrics will always happen. You need Check Metrics complementing your North Star to make sure that the value you create is sustainable. And I suggest that you share the data with everyone so that the whole team can watch out for any problems.

With colorful angry birds looking at us from various angles, Teemu Hämäläinen, product director at Rovio Entertainment in Espoo, Finland, continued relating his stories about the games industry.

The visibility and openness in this industry is fascinating. It's the same within our company. Every week there is a report that goes to every employee, which covers our games and tells us about their successes,

how many users they have, improvements made compared to the previous
week, how they fell back, and so on.

Teemu Hämäläinen, product director at Rovio
Entertainment, Espoo, Finland

At any given time, there is one aspect of your product offering or your business model that deserves paying attention to above everything else. That's your North Star Metric. But your north star is always about results and the information about it may arrive late. That's why you use additional Support Metrics offering you insights earlier, so you can do course corrections faster. Besides that, the focus on one thing doesn't mean you should stop monitoring everything else. By keeping track of multiple Check Metrics, you maintain a fuller understanding of the health of your business.

When you take all this together, you will end up with either an online dashboard or a weekly report of measurements that are crucial for steering your business in the right direction. If you make your team responsible for creating and reviewing that weekly report or dashboard, you might feel like a king and be able to enjoy a worry-free vacation.

For related notes, articles, books, examples, and downloads, check out this web page:
https://startup-scaleup-screwup.com/north-star-metric.

The Entropy Tango

Keep a Product Backlog with Minimum Viable Features and Experiment Stories updated through ongoing Backlog Maintenance.

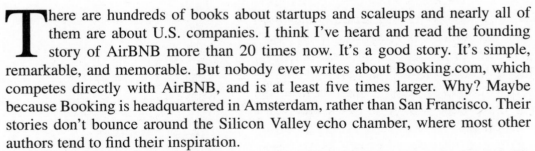

There are hundreds of books about startups and scaleups and nearly all of them are about U.S. companies. I think I've heard and read the founding story of AirBNB more than 20 times now. It's a good story. It's simple, remarkable, and memorable. But nobody ever writes about Booking.com, which competes directly with AirBNB, and is at least five times larger. Why? Maybe because Booking is headquartered in Amsterdam, rather than San Francisco. Their stories don't bounce around the Silicon Valley echo chamber, where most other authors tend to find their inspiration.

And so, I went to Amsterdam to learn from Melanie Wessels, who is an Agile Coach at Booking.com, how her colleagues at the company do their jobs.

> *We want there to be chaos so that teams can innovate and be creative*
> *and have autonomy. But we also want some form of organization so that*

there are boundaries within which the teams can innovate. So, there are a couple of things we consider required for all teams. We call them the Booking Agile Essentials. Three of the items are the Agile Retrospective, the Daily Standup, and having a Product Backlog. These are the three practices that we say every team needs to have.

Melanie Wessels, Agile Coach at Booking.com,
Amsterdam, The Netherlands

I love backlogs. I make backlogs of many things. For example, one of my hobbies is keeping track of popular, best-rated, and award-winning science fiction and fantasy books. I enjoy browsing specialized websites to find interesting books that I wasn't aware of and then documenting their titles, authors, release dates, and book series. As a result of this, I have nearly 4,000 books on my reading backlog. I treat them as options or suggestions for later reading. You might also call it my wish list. It's a wish list because I am fully aware that I won't be able to buy and read all those books. I have many other things to do. I also have a list of more than 1,000 places to see before I die. And I'm working on a backlog of the craziest, most time-wasting backlogs.

All backlogs should be treated in a similar manner, whether they are Product Backlogs, Content Backlogs, Improvement Backlogs, or any other list of unscheduled work items. They are *wish lists*, not *to-do lists*. In project management literature, the Product Backlog is often defined as "a list of features *needed* in the product" (a to-do list). But that definition is wrong. The backlog is a list of features *desired* in a product (a wish list). Your appetite is always larger than your capacity. I desire to read 4,000 books and see 1,000 places around the world, but I know neither will ever happen. There's not enough capacity in my life

to accommodate my limitless appetite for reading and travel. Likewise, many features on a Product Backlog will not be implemented because we always have more ideas and requirements than we can ever hope to realize. The Product Backlog is a tool that typically fits in the Hypothesize stream of the Innovation Vortex because it's about the collection of ideas that might be worthy of implementation.

Sergei Anikin, CTO at Pipedrive in Tallinn, Estonia, told me how his teams also rely on Product Backlogs and other Scrum practices.

> *We just went with the standard Scrum process, which is very well defined. There's no need to spend energy on explaining what it is. You get a book or invite an agile coach, and everyone understands, more or less, what the responsibilities are. To start, you really just implement the process, focus on the feedback loop, and have all the required roles and artifacts in place. You can't start a team without having a product manager and product backlog. Sometimes people say, "Okay, let's do Scrum and here are the engineers." But the founders don't make time to actually put some effort into forming a Product Backlog, and then the teams don't know what to do.*
>
> *Sergei Anikin, CTO at Pipedrive, Tallinn, Estonia*

Startups and scaleups need backlogs like kids and adults need education. Just like Booking and Pipedrive, my team has a Product Backlog, too. We use it to add ideas that might boost our North Star Metric. We use it to correlate features with our Value Proposition Wheel. We even added some thoughts about an iOS version of the app (for later, obviously). We maintain such a wish list because it's a waste of our mental capacity to keep all good suggestions in our heads. When I order a new book, I pick one from my curated wish list. I don't waste my time trying to recall thousands of earlier suggestions. Similarly, when we pick new features to be scheduled, we prefer to go to our Product Backlog rather than the collective memories of the team.

Product Backlogs exist in many forms. There are countless professional tools available that enable you to create and maintain backlogs. But you can just as well use a simple document, a database, sticky notes on a wall, or index cards in a file system. Depending on the tool of your choice, you can prioritize feature ideas according to various criteria, cluster features into logical groupings, and make sure that the suggestions on the list are cohesive and fit the Product Vision.

Not long after the successful closure of the Equity Crowdfunding, when our team was together for a team offsite in warm Barcelona in spring, we decided that we needed a new deadline. The crowdfunding campaign had worked well as a way to focus our efforts as a team. After the money was in, we missed having a concrete date to work toward and keep our ourselves organized. A North Star Metric helps us to keep focus on certain areas. But a deadline helps us to maintain a sense of urgency. We decided that the big Agile2018 conference in San Diego, where I was invited to speak after the summer, would be our next major milestone. Project San Diego was born.

To kick off Project San Diego, I created a new backlog as a two-dimensional spreadsheet. The columns listed different areas of our platform (such as *menu*, *users*, *practices*, and *guides*) and the rows showed different user behaviors (such as *searching*, *sharing*, and *rating*). By ex-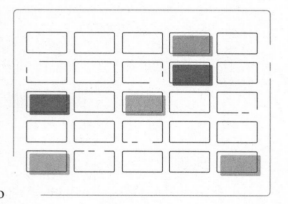amining each cell in the spreadsheet, I was able to explore many feature ideas that would achieve consistency across our platform if we implemented them across an entire row or along an entire column. (For example, what are all the areas in which we want to search? And what are all the user behaviors that we need for guides?) I assigned an urgency (high, medium, low) and a level of importance (one or two points) to each cell in the spreadsheet. The Product Backlog looked complicated, but the system was actually quite simple. Each week, the team scored 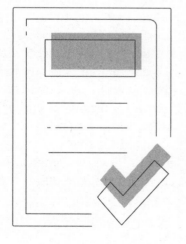points depending on how much of the features they were able to complete. With a weekly Burn Chart, we could monitor the trend line of points that we earned, which gave us a sense of progress toward the deadline of the project (see Chapter 14).

On your Product Backlog, you describe your feature ideas as User Stories. A User Story is just a short and simple description of a feature *told from the perspective of the person who wants that feature*, normally a user. For every User Story, it makes sense to document the Lean Persona and the part of the Value Proposition Wheel you are addressing with the desired feature.

Some experts suggest distinguishing between Minimum Marketable Features (MMFs) and ordinary User Stories. Authors Mark Denne and Jane Cleland-Huang defined an MMF as the smallest unit of functionality that has intrinsic market value. The description of an MMF should focus on the benefits that a user will enjoy as a result of this feature and on the acceptance criteria that will allow you to check whether these benefits have indeed been achieved. You can think of MMFs as any features that you would gladly announce to your customers in a blog post, in your newsletter, or (for those less than half my age) in a Snapchat or Instagram video. When something is not worth announcing, it could be a lower-level feature that is part of a (larger) MMF.

Another type of item on your Product Backlog is the Lean Experiment or Experiment Story. Lean Experiments are hypotheses of value that you want to have tested. When you move experiments from your Product Backlog to your Kanban Board, remember that the Experiment Stories cannot be considered done until their hypotheses have been validated. To do this, your team will need to apply some tools for validated learning, such as Customer Interviews or Split Tests.

Together, experiments and features should form the majority of items on your Product Backlog. With experiments, your team's focus is on learning and doing the right thing. With features, your team's goal is productivity and doing things right. A download button that only measures whether customers are interested in downloading a product counts as an experiment. The actual implementation of the download process counts as a feature.

There are still other kinds of items that can go on a Product Backlog: bug reports, team requests, improvement stories, technical work, research spikes, kudo cards, and more. As long as a smart, self-organizing team optimizes their productivity (with features) and learning (with experiments), it is up to them to decide how to keep track of all other things they need to do. Teams at different companies go about it in different ways, as my interview partners at TransferWise and Taxify revealed.

Jeff McClelland is people experience lead at TransferWise, in Tallinn. Jeff shared with me how TransferWise has for a long time leaned toward features over architecture.

> *We've been around for about seven years and we were always very product/customer-focused. We've always tried to move very fast and in many directions. So, product-wise, we actually have a really simple product, but we've been trying to conquer many new geographies. In every country, we needed to find a local bank. We needed to work with the local regulators. We also needed to do all the technical work with those banks and every bank is different from all the previous ones. That meant that we've always been building a lot of stuff from scratch, and it's the same with all these payment methods that we have started to support. Technically, we ran the risk of building a house of cards. We put all our energy into working as fast as we could to deliver what our customers wanted. But in the end, it's bitten us, actually. We are now investing a lot of energy in fixing our legacy code and pulling things out of this monolith database and into microservices. We could certainly have done that earlier. We now have to pull out a lot of engineering time and slow ourselves down to build a better foundation in a way that will support us in the next five years. I suppose all companies struggle with these kinds of decisions: when to go fast and expand, and when to slow down and stabilize.*
>
> *Jeff McClelland, people experience lead at TransferWise,*
> *Tallinn, Estonia*

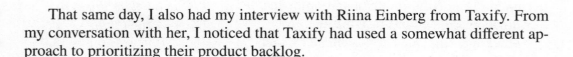

That same day, I also had my interview with Riina Einberg from Taxify. From my conversation with her, I noticed that Taxify had used a somewhat different approach to prioritizing their product backlog.

> *A key component is to automate as much as possible. Don't just hire bodies to cover some crap you have coded or that you haven't figured out yet. But think smart and automate as much as you can because this keeps your head count down and keeps people motivated. People are not interested in dealing with crap. They are not interested in dealing with legacy code. They*

are much more interested in building new stuff and building smart things rather than fixing stuff. We even automate our customer support. We pick people who are not just answering tickets with some manual or something, but we hire people who constantly think, "Okay, we have these questions from clients. How we can improve things? What can we automate next?" This is something very common for Estonian startups specifically because our resources are limited. We don't have the possibilities that startups in some other countries have where they can just find hundreds and hundreds of new hires. We have to deal with the problem of having only a limited number of people here. And therefore, we try to be smart.

Riina Einberg, general manager at Taxify, Tallinn, Estonia

Clearly, prioritization of new features versus architectural work is something that startups and scaleups handle in different ways. Some lean toward more features first, others lean toward automation first. In the end, it all needs to be balanced and all decisions depend on context.

A similar backlog prioritization challenge was revealed to me by Patrick Kua, who I met years ago at an agile conference in London. It was a pleasure to see him again as CTO of mobile banking provider N26 in Berlin. Patrick told me how he had to deal with the prioritization of business requests for his product teams.

When a company grows, every part of the company wants to grow at a similar pace. But it's often harder to find people in engineering than in other areas of the business. This easily leads to the organization screwing things up. There will be a lot of tension in the company because the business side is growing faster than the engineering side, and a lot of people are always requesting stuff from the engineers. Without visualizing the product development pipeline, you have incoming hidden demand that comes in through software developers who say, "Okay, we'll do this," or through infrastructure people who say, "Sure, I'll take care of that." And then, at some point, they wonder which priority should I be working on? And that causes natural tension. At our company, I try to make sure that we have a better prioritization process where we have clarity as to where things sit so that people can, once again, focus on what's most important.

Patrick Kua, CTO at N26, Berlin, Germany

When you have a Product Backlog full of Minimum Marketable Features, User Stories, Experiment Stories, and other items, you need a way to prioritize what to do next. When the chosen tool and your time allow it, you can go crazy and add different values to your backlog items, such as Risk Level, Time Criticality, Business Value, Cost of Delay, and Job Size. On a regular basis, you could use a formula such as Business Value divided by Job Size, or Cost of Delay divided by Job Size, to find the backlog items with the highest priorities.

Such prioritization would not be much different from me calculating the books to read next by using a formula that includes the number of awards, average rating, number of reviews, publication date, and so on. (I don't have such a formula yet, but I'm loony enough to devise one.) However, most of the time, practical concerns determine the book I read next. When I travel, it needs to be a book that is light and easy to pack. During the long summer days and winter nights, I prefer voluminous, epic series. And for variety, each next book should be of a different type than the previous one.

With product backlogs, it is often the same. You can calculate formulas all you want, but most of the time, practical concerns such as the next milestone, a press release, a funding round, the mood of the team, and variety of work are better indicators of what features and experiments to prioritize next.

Backlog Maintenance is the habit of paying continuous attention to your wish list. Updating the items, refreshing the information, and changing priorities according to either a formula or practical concerns, should be a regular job. The top of your backlog, ordered by highest priorities, deserves most of your time. Make those top items as small, as detailed, and as clear as the team will need, just before transferring them to the team's Kanban Board. A bit further down the list, where the priorities are lower, the items can be more coarse-grained, and the type of maintenance should be less frequent and will require less effort. At the low end of the backlog, maintenance typically just means dumping and categorizing large, unpolished ideas, and throwing them out when they've been floating around there for too long and are not able to climb their way up.

Teemu Hämäläinen, product director at Rovio, continued relating his stories about the gaming industry.

With our game, we're building a hobby product. And in order to keep the game competitive, we need to offer fresh and new things to our players frequently. That is the show we are running and we're running it with 15 to 20 people. And as a team, we need to understand who we are competing against every day in the entertainment industry. We need to follow those products and understand in which direction they are evolving, and we need to keep up. Sometimes, in a very rapid phase, within a few months, there might be some new product that some other publisher has released that is based on the same rules, but it has changed some of the fundamentals. And then we need to ask ourselves, "Can we adapt to that with our current game? Or is it something that is going to be in our next product?" In our business, there needs to be a lot of adaptation and a very high learning speed, to operate the kind of games that we have.

Teemu Hämäläinen, product director at Rovio Entertainment,
Espoo, Finland

After the interview at Rovio, on my way out, I couldn't resist taking a picture of myself and a giant red angry bird, evidence of the staggering learning curve of the company.

Your Product Backlog is a living document. It keeps evolving as your product and the environment in which it will be used evolve. This is why I think that the original term *backlog refinement* is a bad term. On the one hand, you put in work to add details, estimates, and priorities to the backlog items (refinement). On the other hand, anything that you don't pay attention to gets stale, old, and out-of-date (entropy). The bigger your Product Backlog, the more refinement you need to do just to keep up with the entropy.

Backlog Maintenance is like an everlasting dance between order and chaos. The result of the dance is not more and more certainty but just keeping up with ongoing change. When you realize that you're actually doing maintenance, you might become more critical of all those feature ideas that will never get done. You may even want to consider cleaning out your wish list every now and then. As I recently did with a few of those 4,000 book titles.

For related notes, articles, books, examples, and downloads, check out this web page: https://startup-scaleup-screwup.com/product-backlog.

A Pleasure to Burn

Keep an eye on your progress with Burn-down Charts, Burn-up Charts, or Cumulative Flow Diagrams.

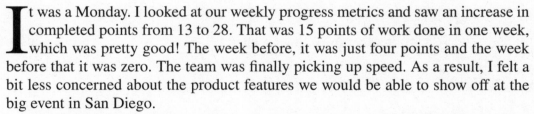

It was a Monday. I looked at our weekly progress metrics and saw an increase in completed points from 13 to 28. That was 15 points of work done in one week, which was pretty good! The week before, it was just four points and the week before that it was zero. The team was finally picking up speed. As a result, I felt a bit less concerned about the product features we would be able to show off at the big event in San Diego.

Our measurement of the amount of work done was quite simple. We had our Product Backlog spreadsheet with many cells showing a priority for urgency and some points for importance. One point for regular features, two points for the most valuable ones. That was it. There was no estimation involved or anything complicated. The number of points completed per week was the easiest way for us to measure how much progress we were making toward the public launch of the product, our Project San Diego.

By drawing a simple chart of the points, we completed per week, we could see that we probably wouldn't get everything done but it looked like we would get close. If we could stick to a production speed of around 15 points per week, we would have 150 points done at the time of the launch, which would be 84 percent of our goal. Not perfect by far, but good enough not to feel embarrassed about it. Like the *okonomiyaki* that I've learned to make after my trip to Japan.

A Burn Chart is a diagram of work versus time, which comes in two flavors. Burn-*down* charts show how much work there is still left to do, which means that the trend line goes down, often toward a deadline on the horizontal axis (see Figure 14.1). Burn-*up* charts show how much work has been completed, which means that the trend line goes up, usually toward a total amount of work to be done, on the vertical axis (see Figure 14.2).

Burn-down charts have been popularized by Scrum, a framework for collaborative teams in product development, but some teams prefer burn-up charts because they make it easier to visualize when the scope has changed. In a burn-up chart, a

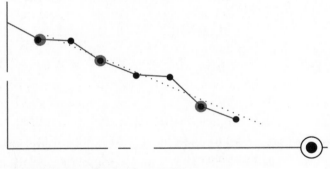

FIGURE 14.1 **Burn-down Chart**

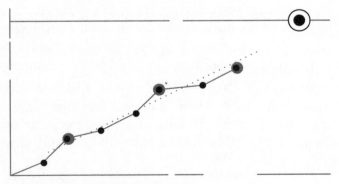

FIGURE 14.2 **Burn-up Chart**

scope increase means that the horizontal line for the total amount of work goes up. When a development team wants to visualize that it has difficulty keeping up with the amount of work that the business keeps throwing at them, the burn-up chart is the better version to choose. Both versions typically fit in the Sensitize stream of the Innovation Vortex because they are about creating awareness of the progress that a team is making.

With both types of Burn Chart, you can measure the amount of work done in points or in features and experiments. Some teams like to estimate the size or value of User Stories and Experiment Stories, but many don't bother and simply count the number of items. My team prefers to distinguish between two or three values that require no further estimation. Each of these approaches can be fine.

Keep your method as simple as you can get away with because experience shows that estimation is usually a waste of (your) time. You get little extra value out of the effort you spend estimating the sizes of work items. If you make all jobs small enough, you can just count the number of things done and the number of things still to do. It's like a cafe counting the number of clients served and the number of clients waiting. Who cares about estimating what each of them wants, how much they will pay, and if they will flirt with the barista?

The amount of work completed per week is often referred to as the *velocity* of the team. The nice thing about Burn Charts is that they help you make a forecast of the amount of work that can be completed in the next few weeks, based on the trend of the velocity in the previous weeks. This means you can also forecast how much of your planned work can be completed before a deadline. If the trend line in the Burn Chart shows that you're not going to make it, it's good to know this as early as possible. It will allow you to update your plans. This is why the Burn Chart is best updated regularly, before your Daily Stand-ups, Daily Cafes, or weekly planning meetings. With one simple graph, you can see how much work was done per week, how much there is still remaining, and how much you can expect to have completed.

You can use Burn Charts for many things, far beyond the development of a product. I could draw a Burn Chart right now showing all the work that I do to complete this book. I had a burn-up chart for our Equity Crowdfunding campaign, showing the amount of money committed by investors. I could also make a burn-down chart picturing the amount of cash that we have in our bank account, which would look eerily similar to a sumo wrestler tumbling down Mount Fuji. Interestingly, the amount of cash that startups spend per month is actually called their *burn rate*. When you're burning money anyway, you might as well visualize that on a Burn Chart!

We can further improve the usefulness of Burn Charts by adding a bit more information to them. Normally, there is only one line of completed items on a standard burn-up chart. That line shows the total amount of work that has the final status *done*. When something is only half done (or half-written, or half-committed, or half-spent), it doesn't count toward progress on the Burn Chart. Only completed stuff counts as done. However, when you have different statuses in your workflow, possibly managed with a Kanban Board, you can show those statuses individually on the same diagram by using multiple lines. The burn-up chart then becomes what we refer to as a Cumulative Flow Diagram (CFD). (See Figure 14.3.)

You can easily create a CFD based on the workflow on a Kanban Board. With each status, you count the total number of items (or the sum of their sizes or values) that have successfully arrived at that point. You then plot each of them as a stacked diagram and you draw their lines in different colors. The burn-up chart that we discussed before is actually nothing more than a simple CFD that shows you just two statuses: the amount of work *planned* and the amount of work *completed*. But in between planned and completed, you can identify and visualize any number of statuses, giving you more in-depth information about the pipeline of your work.

There are a couple more interesting things that you can learn from CFDs. At any given moment, if you look at the *vertical* space between two lines, it shows you the amount of work in progress or Queue Length in that particular stage. If you look at the *horizontal* space between two lines, you get an idea of how much time it roughly takes to move an item from one stage to the other (sometimes referred to as Cycle Time or Operations Time). If you look at the horizontal space between both outermost lines, you see how much time it takes from the moment an item is offered to the team until it is fully done (often referred to as Lead Time or Tactical Time). Additionally, like the burn-up chart, which is just its simpler brother, the CFD also shows you the entire scope of the work, which is the line that's floating above all the others.

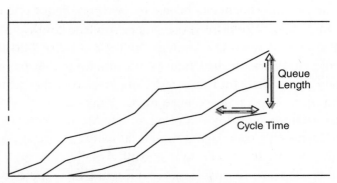

FIGURE 14.3 Cumulative Flow Diagram

When you draw a Cumulative Flow Diagram on a regular basis, you can see patterns and possible issues concerning the workload of your team. It is a great tool to examine just before Daily Stand-ups, Daily Cafes, or weekly planning meetings, because it helps your team to reflect on their workflow. Apart from scope creep challenges, they might identify slow progress, bottlenecks, long turnaround times, and other productivity issues that they will need to discuss. However, don't believe that a CFD is going to solve any problems. It merely helps you gain better insights into what's happening.

So, what is the best tool for your team? The Burn Chart or the Cumulative Flow Diagram? As long as your business is still in startup mode, it makes sense to keep things simple, as I do, by just calculating points completed per week and drawing a simple line that goes up or down. These Burn Charts are easy to make, and they are easy to understand for everyone. But when your business accelerates into scaling mode, and you spend more time on stabilizing and professionalizing your processes, it would be a smart idea to turn your charts into full-blown CFDs. They are more advanced than Burn Charts and give you a lot more information.

It was a Thursday. At a startup event in Helsinki, I interviewed a few dozen startup founders and asked them about their struggles and biggest challenges as entrepreneurs and business leaders. Several of them indicated that the turbulence of their work-lives, and the ups and downs of the business, were very hard to get used to. "If there's one thing you should write in your book," one of them said, "it's that startup life is so dynamic that you can experience the highs and lows on just one day."

I very much enjoyed those conversations I had that day, recognizing many founder problems and experiences, but also feeling that I had everything well under control. We still had plenty of money in the bank; my team was making good progress toward Project San Diego; I was making decent headway with my book; all Burn Charts looked like impressive mountain sides, and Helsinki was sunnier than I had ever experienced. It was the perfect day for one of my software developers to send me an urgent message saying, "Can we talk?"

An hour later, over a video call back at my hotel, one of our most productive team members told me that he had received a job offer that he simply couldn't refuse. He was leaving our team. I foresaw a terrible effect on our Burn Chart.

For related notes, articles, books, examples, and downloads, check out this web page: https://startup-scaleup-screwup.com/burn-charts.

The New Recruit

Get your hiring process in order with a Recruitment Funnel, sourcing by the founders, and some Skills Tests and Work Samples.

Okay, that hurt. A great team member quitting, because he received a better offer elsewhere, is never an enjoyable thing. But in our case, with a team of just a handful of people, and a Burn Chart that showed it was difficult enough already to get most of our work done before the Project San Diego deadline, it was really quite painful.

Whatever happens, don't panic. That's what I tell myself at least 42 times per year. So, I didn't.

I discussed the unfortunate situation with the rest of the team during our next Daily Cafe. They all felt the impact. The thing I feared most was that it might de-motivate some of the others and start a domino effect that could wipe out our team until I had nobody left. Fortunately, this didn't happen. In fact, the team came back to me a day later and said, "We discussed it. We like the project, we love our work, and we enjoy this team. We've decided to stick to the goal and release a public version before the deadline." The pain of the departure of one member pulled the rest of the team closer together.

We discussed the Project Backlog, reprioritized features, and committed to a trimmed-down release that would still be doable and acceptable. And I felt proud of our little company. If we ever manage to create a Culture Code book or slide deck, this is a story that I will want to have included.

Perhaps it is easier for me than for others. As an author and public speaker, I regularly get people asking me if I have a job for them. Usually, I don't. But it means that recruitment of new team members is slightly less difficult for me than it is for others. And still, I find it hard. I fully appreciate the struggles that other entrepreneurs and business leaders are faced with when they are trying to form a team, or trying to repair one.

"Hire only the best," is what you read all the time in startup blogs and magazines, which is easy to say, but not so easy to do. At the event in Helsinki, during my conversations with fellow founders, many of them said that getting a team was even harder than getting funding. They said it was their number one challenge. And most had no experience at all in recruitment.

The simple truth is that startups have to do a better job than established businesses setting up a recruitment process for scouting, attracting, and evaluating candidates. This is doable. What traditional companies offer is a good salary, job security, and an employee handbook of 300 pages. What startup founders can offer is an exciting adventure, a great team, and a Culture Book full of stories-yet-to-be-written. From my personal experience, I know that there are many great talents willing to exchange money and safety for personal growth and professional friendships.

A Recruitment Funnel costs effort and dedication, which is something that most founders don't invest nearly enough time in. But the Key Resources piece on your Shiftup Business Quilt needs attention and the Team slide on your Pitch Deck needs to look impressive. As a founder, entrepreneur, or business leader, you had better learn how to do recruitment well.

Kristjan Koik, founder and CEO at Flender, explained to me the challenges of recruitment in a popular tech hub such as Dublin, Ireland. The offices of Flender were so new that the walls were still crisp and empty.

Accenture is just next door. They are massive, with 2,000 people, I think. Then there's Google over there, with 6,000 Google heads. And Facebook is just there on the left. Another massive building. You can imagine how hard recruitment is when you're a scaleup in a place like this. Why would anybody come here when they can have free lunches and free massages everywhere else? Well, one of the main things that drives them to us is that they can learn and grow a lot quicker in our company. With us, they have a chance to do things that they would never get to do over there. In our company, they get exposed to things that they would normally never experience if they were employee number 1,806. Our head of credit is a great example. He worked at the biggest bank in Ireland and he came to work with us for less salary than he was getting, and with practically no benefits, since we're a scaleup. And he's not just one in a million, but all the others are like that. They join because they know they can make a difference. And they will learn a lot.

Kristjan Koik, founder and CEO at Flender, Dublin, Ireland

The number one recruitment rule for founders is, "Don't delegate the responsibility to recruitment firms or HR departments." Startups should do it all themselves! I don't know any startup that had great success with external recruiters in the early stages of their business. As a business leader, you need to learn how to become a great recruiter yourself. Good talent is the blood of your business, so don't make someone else responsible for supplying it. Don't ask recruiters, HR professionals, or outsourcing businesses to find a team for you. Your business will be a product of what you prioritize. Therefore, when the business is still young, you should prioritize spending a significant amount of time on the hiring process. Some even suggest that you should Always Be Hiring (ABH). The best leaders are those who understand that growing teams is as important as building products.

Only when your business shifts up to the Acceleration Stage (6), and you have learned how to manage a great Recruitment Funnel, you will have to delegate finding new talent to others. From that stage, it might be best if you get yourself a full-time recruiter who will bring the process to the next higher level. External recruitment firms can play a role for very specific jobs and rare, expensive talent. But even when you're scaling up, I'd say most of your recruitment work, like most of your product development work, is best done in-house.

In Kraków, Poland, Michał Borkowski, founder and CEO of Brainly, told me that, even when scaling up, the final responsibility still remains with the managers.

Great HR is there to help managers hire better. They don't replace managers in the hiring process. It's the manager's job to hire the best people. Human Resources is just there to help and support, not the other way around. I think it is one of the dangers for scaleups that they often screw up when they implement HR in the company. The leaders and managers stop thinking about bringing in new people. They think, from that moment on, HR should deliver all the candidates. But it doesn't work like that because everybody can go and work in 500 different places. The market is just so competitive out there. The ones that need to stand out and capture the attention of great talents are the leaders of the business.
    Michał Borkowski, founder and CEO of Brainly, Kraków, Poland

Similar to sales and funding, a hiring process works as a funnel. The goal of the Recruitment Funnel (see Figure 15.1) is to find many prospects and to identify as early as possible which of those are high-quality candidates. The fewer people move to the next stages in the funnel, the less you waste your time on unqualified candidates. This

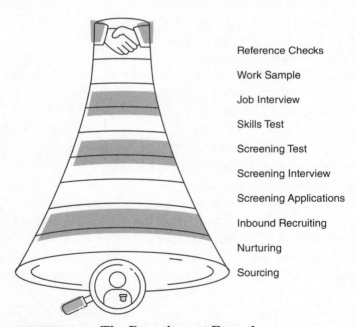

FIGURE 15.1 **The Recruitment Funnel**

Reference Checks

Work Sample

Job Interview

Skills Test

Screening Test

Screening Interview

Screening Applications

Inbound Recruiting

Nurturing

Sourcing

hiring process is one of the first processes that you will want to document. The reason is that it needs to become efficient and effective earlier than most other processes in your business. It is typically something that you want to have nailed down even before you enter the Stabilization stage (5) of the Business Lifecycle. It doesn't matter if the process is a simple Google document or an Excel spreadsheet, as long as everyone on your team understands how it is supposed to work and how they can contribute to finding great candidates.

At the top of the funnel, we find the **Sourcing** step, which is possibly the hardest part of recruiting. Many organizations rely on ads and postings on job boards and recruitment websites, but the truly great talents are usually not looking for a good job. They already have one. However, some of them are willing to consider switching to an interesting alternative, as I have painfully noticed myself. We call them passive candidates. Your job  as an entrepreneur or intrapreneur is to find these passive candidates and make them aware that a job at your startup could be more interesting than what they have now. Fortunately, there are thousands of passive candidates waiting to be wooed and plucked away from the embrace of their unfortunate managers. The trick is figuring out how.

The best source of passive candidates is undoubtedly the aggregate of the personal networks of your current team members. Everyone knows some people who are not 100 percent happy and engaged in their current jobs but who haven't taken any concrete steps to find alternatives. It will be just a matter of reaching out and saying, "Hey, how's your job?" and "Let me tell you about mine."

> *It's mostly our friends and their friends. So we use internal networks. I would say more than 60 percent of our new recruitments come from our internal networks.*
>
> *Petri Haapio, partner at Reaktor, Helsinki, Finland*

Petri Haapio, partner at Reaktor in Helsinki agreed with me when we were chatting on the company's roof terrace, overlooking the city of Helsinki. I found the same sentiment in several other interviews.

The next best source for new candidates is the many social networks and community websites that the Internet has to offer, such as LinkedIn (for sales and business), Facebook (for marketing), GitHub and StackOverflow (for developers), Behance (for designers), AngelList and Hacker News (for startup enthusiasts), Reddit and Quora (for geeks and specialists), and many, many more. Figure out in which online niche your preferred candidates could be roaming around, enter that space, and start a conversation with the smartest and most active members. Don't. Spam. Them! Just talk with them about their profession. What is the worst thing that could happen? That they tell you they already have a great job when you let it slip that you have an open position? So? Congratulate them and move on.

After sourcing comes **Nurturing**. Use a Trello board, an Airtable database, or a more advanced contact management system, to keep track of all the interesting people that you encounter. The ones you find are prospects that should go into your nurturing bucket. Nurturing only works when you invest in personal and meaningful conversations with your prospects. Don't just send them promotional e-mails. Don't just tell them, "I want to hire you!" Reply  to their social network updates, add a comment to their latest blog post or video, or ask them a question within their preferred community. True engagement starts with conversation, not promotion. Do this with care and restraint. There is a delicate line between a respectful suitor and a stalking creep. To do this well, you need to set aside a few hours per week for these nurturing activities.

When a passive candidate shows any interest in the job opportunities you have available, and is willing to talk, it is highly likely that you will spend the first part of the process selling your business to them. Remember, these are passive candidates. You first need to convince *them* that a job switch is worth considering. Make sure your Content Calendar has some blog posts scheduled that interested job candidates will see first when they check out your website.

The next step is **Inbound Recruiting**, which is about being interesting in as many places as possible. And I don't mean plastering the Internet with your job vacancies. What I mean is that, through a smart strategy with your Content Calendar, consumers of your blog posts, articles, or videos could develop an interest in what you're doing as a business. Some of those will want to know more. You can turn those passive candidates,  who weren't even thinking about quitting their jobs, into active candidates, who realize that the work you are doing is more interesting than the work they currently have. If they share the same passion as you do, it will be a lot easier to persuade them to make the leap.

In the previous steps, you did your best to turn passive candidates into active candidates. Once such people express interest in a job, you will ask them to supply some information about themselves, and then the following steps in the hiring process are pretty standard across most companies. I'm sure you will recognize them easily.

In the **Screening Applications** step, it is crucial that you identify the misfits. The earlier you dismiss unqualified candidates, the less time you waste in the following steps of the funnel. For example, you may want to ensure that candidates have the right language skills, that they know what type of business you are and what role they are applying for, and that they will be available when you need them. You will want to see positive evaluations  of these issues based on the materials they submit, such as a CV, an application letter, or an application video.

The **Screening Interview** can take place remotely on Zoom or Skype or some other video conferencing tool and often takes less than 20 minutes. It is meant to get more certainty about basic qualifications that are hard to evaluate from just reading or viewing the job applications. You can check if the candidates understand the risk and uncertainty of working  at a startup business, and you can test if their value system is similar to yours. You can also use this step to assess whether the candidate has had a serious look at the company and has prepared some good questions about the role and the hiring process.

Before continuing with the deeper interviews, I recommend that you ask job candidates to participate in a **Skills Test**. Give them a small assignment or a practical task related to the job so that you can quickly weed out the ones who were able to bluff themselves through the job application and the screening steps.

I once interviewed software developers who had never heard of concepts such as test-driven development or microservices, which I consider elementary concepts for programmers and software engineers. The waste of my time was completely my own fault and you have a similar responsibility for your time. Why would you schedule long interviews with people who don't even know the basic terminology of their job? By the time you get to the actual job interview, you should already have narrowed down the list to skilled candidates who know their trade, unless you consider it acceptable that you educate them on the job.

The **Job Interview** step can be broken down into multiple consecutive interviews. If you did your homework well, you have prepared a Hiring Scorecard, which I will discuss in the next chapter, and you've broken up the qualifications that you should seek evidence for into different sessions. My team has two interview sessions with our candidates: one with the exec-  utive (that would be me) and one with other team members (without me). We aim to check for different qualities in these two sessions, which we have defined on the Hiring Scorecard. Other companies organize three or even more separate interviews, but I think you shouldn't overdo it. The law of diminishing returns suggests that each additional interview will be less valuable than the previous one, while the costs of organizing them remain the same.

Before the final interview, I recommend asking job candidates for a **Work Sample**. This means getting them to actually do a bit of work on your product for a few hours, preferably together with one or two other team members. Real work is the best predictor of how someone will perform on a job.

It is a sign of goodwill to pay your job candidates for these few hours of work, but in my experience, no job candidate is really interested in payment at this point. If they are any good then the only thing that will interest them is enjoying the actual work and proving that they deserve to be on your team. Everything else will be of secondary concern. But you might want to pay them anyway.

Finally, you may want to end your hiring process with **Reference Checks**. Personally, I've always had some doubts about asking a job candidate's former managers and colleagues about their experiences working with that candidate. Perfor-  mance is a product of a person and his or her environment, which means that any feedback you get tells you as much about the candidate's former employer as it does about the job can- didate herself. But still, I found that many business leaders who are smarter than I am find reference checks to be an important part of the hiring process. I guess that asking former colleagues a couple of questions (with the consent of the candidate) won't hurt anyone. Just don't forget there are always multiple perspectives and in- terpretations for each story that you will hear.

The entire hiring process needs to be monitored carefully and you may want to delegate the management of the Recruitment Funnel to some of your other team members. As a founder and business leader, you should spend most of your time at the start of the funnel, engaging in conversations with dozens of passive candidates who had never before heard about your business. It's a lot of work, for sure. But once you have a great hiring process set up, which promises to be a good experience for both parties, the sourcing of new candidates could be an enjoyable way of spending some of your time.

Let me emphasize that last bit once more. Don't ever make the mistake of thinking that the hiring process is just about you and your company. At every stage of the Recruitment Funnel, you need to ensure that the process is a great experience for your job candidates, too. Even when you reject them (or when *they* reject *you*), you want these people to have a good opinion of your company. If they are not a good match for you (or you are not a good match for them), they might still have some friends they could recommend. Always try to be a great company for everyone, including the ones you don't hire, and including the ones who quit your team to move elsewhere. Who knows? If you stay nice, they might send you a replacement later. Maybe. Someday.

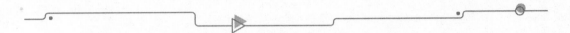

For related notes, articles, books, examples, and downloads, check out this web page: https://startup-scaleup-screwup.com/recruitment-funnel.

The Enigma Score

Start workforce planning and talent management in your business with Hiring Scorecards that help you avoid culture misfits.

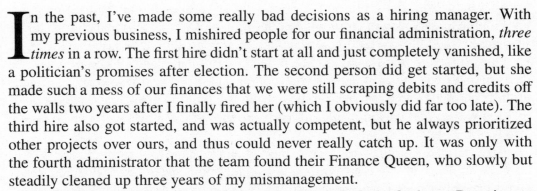

In the past, I've made some really bad decisions as a hiring manager. With my previous business, I mishired people for our financial administration, *three times* in a row. The first hire didn't start at all and just completely vanished, like a politician's promises after election. The second person did get started, but she made such a mess of our finances that we were still scraping debits and credits off the walls two years after I finally fired her (which I obviously did far too late). The third hire also got started, and was actually competent, but he always prioritized other projects over ours, and thus could never really catch up. It was only with the fourth administrator that the team found their Finance Queen, who slowly but steadily cleaned up three years of my mismanagement.

I blame my misadventures as a hiring manager on the lack of a decent Recruitment Funnel, a good Hiring Scorecard, and effective Job Interviews. I always hired people who *seemed* likeable and competent. Sometimes, I was lucky; sometimes I wasn't.

With my current startup, I improved my approach because I was tired of hoping for the best. I decided to upgrade my hiring process and I suggest you do the same. Thoughts and prayers are only good for those who are unwilling to face reality and fix problems.

With every new person added to your team, you change the team's quality, capabilities, trust level, and culture. The smaller the team, the bigger the impact of a mismatch. Some of the top reasons for screwups among new businesses are not having the right team and disharmony among team members. You can prevent much of that through better hiring practices.

The creation of a Hiring Scorecard starts with a vision of what you want your team to be like. Envisioning an ideal picture of your team in the near future is what some would call workforce planning or talent management. What would be the ideal team composition? What are their desired skills and habits? What should they achieve? The result of your thinking should be a list of qualities that new job candidates must be tested for. Some of these qualities will be mentioned in the job description. All of them should end up on the Hiring Scorecard.

An effective search for a good job candidate requires cutting away many un-qualified candidates as quickly as possible. Each desirable quality for job candidates is one that must attract some people but also repel others. The result of each test should be that the group is split in two parts, the pluses and the minuses, with plenty of candidates on the minus side. For example, the quality "team player" is rather useless because almost everyone who is not a solo book author wants to be recognized as a team player. This test doesn't split the group in two. "Radically open and transparent" is a more effective requirement. I know that quite a few candidates are not able (or not even willing) to qualify. You can turn this requirement into a good test that helps split the group in two. In a similar way, each quality that you come up with must assist you in cutting the pool of job candidates into two chunks, those who qualify and those who don't, of which the second should be large.

One challenge that hiring managers have is to plan ahead. When you assume that a person will be working for your company for the next few years, you need to find candidates who can handle the current job *and* the growth and evolution of that job within that period of time. Ideally, you don't just hire for the present; you also hire for the near future.

For example, a product designer in the Validation stage (5) of your business must have the skills to rapidly create different design options for different features, easily revert on earlier decisions, and be willing to accept that many of her designs will not survive for long. But a product designer in the Stabilization stage (6) must be able to create a design vision, develop templates and guidelines, and manage other team members so that they rapidly produce more and more features that adhere to a consistent design. The desirable qualities of a great designer depend on the stage that your startup or scaleup is in. The same applies to almost any other team member.

Keeping your scorecards up-to-date with the constant evolution and growth of your business is not an easy thing to do. More often than not, you should hire people for their current qualities but also for their future potential, so that they can grow along with your business. Likewise, there are talented people you should probably *not* hire yet, because they cannot create value in the current stage that you are in, and you haven't yet reached the stage where their talents will be needed.

At N26 in Berlin, CTO Patrick Kua continued sharing his insights on how he manages the technical side of the company.

> *We had to come up with clever ways of scaling ourselves. That's the challenge of any startup as they grow a customer base. How to scale? In a lot of organizations—particularly banks—they hire people who control the processes and they hire other people to follow those processes. But we have invested a lot in continuous delivery pipelines where we have many automated quality gates. Nothing goes into production if it doesn't pass the gates. At a normal bank, such a gate is usually a person. And people make mistakes, so there are no guarantees. But computers don't make mistakes following the processes that they are given. With infrastructure as code, which is how we manage all our servers, everything is controlled. We can pervert things; we can test things, we can see which changes work and which ones don't, and we can roll things back. It's that capability that a lot of people don't really think about, but it's actually really important. If you want to scale, that's the kind of skill you need to hire for.*
>
> *Patrick Kua, CTO at N26, Berlin, Germany*

The scorecard for my team consists of three kinds of qualities. *Skills* refer to abilities and expertise, the things that people can learn, such as English speaking and writing skills, remote working skills, and concrete experience in our business domain. *Traits* are about personality and attitude, the things that people develop while growing up, such as integrity, patience, openness, and humor. *Attributes* include all other circumstances or situational qualities that might be relevant to the job or to the team, such as cultural background, city of residence, compensation requirements, and availability per week. Your job as a manager is to design a Hiring

Scorecard covering the skills, traits, and attributes that together paint a picture of an ideal candidate for the stage(s) of your business that he or she will be working in, over the next couple of years.

Regarding the search for specialized skills, your focus is expected to shift over time with the evolution of your business model. In the early stages of your business, from Initiation (1) to Validation (4), you work with probably just a handful of people who need to do everything from UX design to back-end development, and from content marketing to some financial administration. This means that you will probably want generalists with wide skill sets as your earliest team members. From Stabilization (5) and onward, you are more likely to hire specialists who will dive deeper into the various areas that have only been touched upon superficially by the generalists.

When looking for suitable job candidates, many people talk about *cultural fit*, which is a term that is often misunderstood. *Fitting in* is best interpreted as pieces of a puzzle that fit together. The pieces of the puzzle are not the same. In fact, they are all different. But they follow a few shared rules for the edges where they touch each other so that they are able to connect. The faces of the puzzle pieces represent the diversity of skills, traits, and other attributes that you need on a well-formed team. The shared rules for the edges represent the shared values and beliefs of the group that you could define in a Culture Code. Fitting in is not about finding people who are similar; it's about finding those who are compatible. And solving that puzzle can be quite an enigma.

Common suggestions to "hire for culture fit" are often nonsense. Managers say things such as, "We only want people that we would like to have a beer with after work." Well, I was part of such a monoculture once. They all had beer after work on Fridays and I was the only one drinking sugar-free cola. It sucked. When I had to climb over a mountain of beer bottles to fetch my two little soda cans, I felt I had "you don't fit in" written all over me.

Some people prefer coffee, not beer. Or tea. Or pink lemonade. You need to build a team of people with a variety of preferences, some of whom don't even want to drink beers or coffees after work because they prefer to be at home, cuddling with their tortoise. Most people can fit in (and adapt to) almost any culture, if those cultures value diversity and respect people's differences.

Diversity and inclusion are important topics for all organizations, which is why "hire for culture fit" is better reworded as "hire against culture misfit." What we often mean is, "don't hire jerks." It takes just one bad apple to spoil the bunch, and just one crooked puzzle piece to ruin the whole picture. I believe that people "not fitting in" should be an exception, not a default. Just keep the misfits out. With a good, diverse culture, there should be only very few misfits.

Another phrase often heard is "hire for attitude, train for skills." It reflects the idea that people's personality traits are almost impossible to change, while it is a lot easier and cheaper to teach them the skills they need to do their jobs. This seems less of an issue in the early stages of the business when most team members should be generalists and deep skills are not required for most areas as long as the basics are covered. It is then obvious to hire people with great attitudes and agreeable personalities. Only in the later stages of the business, when specialists are needed, hiring managers are sometimes tempted to recruit people with deep expertise and bad attitudes (which easily go hand-in-hand). But when your only options are deep skills plus bad attitude versus shallow skills plus great attitude, your choice should be the latter.

If you organize things well, you have a Recruitment Funnel set up with each potential candidate assigned to one of multiple stages of the hiring process. Unlike customer funnels, in the case of a Recruitment Funnel, you do *not* want as many candidates as possible to move from one stage to the next. You only want the *good* candidates to move up the funnel. That's why you should take care of ordering your Hiring Scorecard in such a way that you test for the right qualities in the right stage. You want to know as early as possible when a candidate is a misfit.

For example, as part of the recruitment process, our team requires that a new candidate submits a brief self-recorded video in which they answer a few questions about themselves. We also want them to upload a written document with a short essay about our product. What we test in this stage are not only English verbal and writing skills but also their interest in our product and their capability of using online tools. When candidates have difficulty making themselves understandable, when they have no clue what kind of job they are applying for, or when they don't even know how to upload a video (it happens), we believe our interview time is better invested in other job candidates.

Creating a Hiring Scorecard is pretty straightforward. You can start with a simple list with a row for each quality to be tested, organized per stage, and several columns for the scores. You can work with a range of values such as, "Strong No," "No," "Mixed," "Yes," and "Strong Yes," or some other scale of your preference. Either way, make sure that you have an extra column for your notes and the documentation of the evidence.

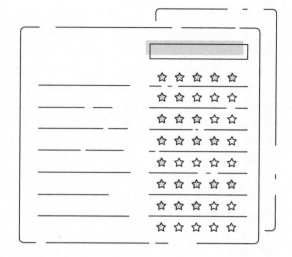

Teach yourself not to give a score to any job candidate, for any quality, without some observed facts supporting your decision. The requirement to provide evidence reduces the chance of bias creeping in. When you hand your Hiring Scorecard to another person on your team, they should be able to see not only how a job candidate scored on the various qualities, but also *why*. Getting multiple team members to interview job candidates and asking them to offer scores independently (with evidence!) also significantly removes bias from your assessments.

If I had used a Hiring Scorecard like this in my earlier management jobs, I'm sure I would have had fewer headaches from team members not showing up, not performing well, or not making any progress. At the very least, I would have had some insights into how team members had passed the tests. Without information, there can be no improvement. In the case of bad hires, if I had used a scorecard, it means I would have had an opportunity to improve the hiring process. And maybe also myself.

For related notes, articles, books, examples, and downloads, check out this web page: https://startup-scaleup-screwup.com/hiring-scorecard.

Standard Hero Behavior

Learn a good approach to Job Interviews using a combination of Behavioral Questions and Behavioral Tests.

Ten years ago, I published a blog post called "100 Interview Questions for Software Developers." I made that list with a friend in an attempt to have better questions for the Job Interviews that I did at the time as a development manager at a software company. It turned out that I was not the only person who needed inspiration for interview questions. Half a million people have flocked to the article since I published it, and 10 years later, it is still the best-viewed post on that blog. Software developers from the other side of the planet told me that they had been interviewed with questions from my blog post, which makes me feel both proud and sad.

In hindsight, I must admit that the questions were not very good. They were all knowledge-oriented questions. It's easy to prepare for knowledge questions in Job Interviews, even for people who are not particularly good at the job they are applying for. With enough preparation, I'm sure I could do well on a knowledge test about vinology, though I never drink any wine. There is a difference between what people say versus what they do. For this reason, some people wonder why companies still put so much effort into traditional Job Interviews when a good amount of research has revealed that interviews with standard questions have very little predictive value.

Unlike all those hiring managers reading my blog, I suggest that you *don't* use your favorite search engine to find "best job interview questions" for your next round of recruitment. It is too tempting to just copy overused but useless questions such as, "How many ping pong balls fit in a truck?" There is a good chance that candidates will have read either my blog post or some of the other popular articles and already know what questions to expect and how to answer them. (They should get a bonus point for the answer, "An American truck or a European truck?")

You should also skip the brain teasers, such as "How many pizzas are sold in London each day?" and skip the cliché questions, such as, "What are your greatest strengths and weaknesses?" and "How do you see yourself five years from now?" These questions usually result in enjoyable conversations and meaningless scores.

The best approach to Job Interviews is to evaluate people based on behaviors, not on conversations. There are two ways of doing this: The first is to ask people questions about their histories and to evaluate them based on stories about their past performance. The second is to give job candidates a score for their *actions* rather than their *answers* in response to your questions and requests.

But first things first. For Job Interviews, you need a structure. Without a structure, it is too easy to let the conversation flow in any direction, which enables the candidate to spend time impressing you with stories that are irrelevant to the job at hand. Without an interview structure, it's also too easy for you to let your personal bias rather than the facts do the scoring for you. Your Job Interviews should all follow the same format, so that you ask the same or similar questions to each candidate. An obvious help here is, of course, a Hiring Scorecard, and I assume that you will create one. During your Job Interviews, zoom in on only the qualities that you are supposed to find evidence for and then ask questions (or make requests) that should generate the information that you need.

Now let's focus on the better questions to ask. Imagine that you want to know if someone is an open and honest person who is not afraid to admit mistakes. The worst questions to ask would be, "Are you an open and honest person?" and "Can you deal with your mistakes?" Quite likely, you will get positive answers from your candidates. That's not because people are lying but because everyone wants to *believe* they are open and honest and able to admit their mistakes. But intentions do not imply behaviors.

A better question would be, "Tell me about a time when you made a bad mistake and you came clean about it with your colleagues. What happened and what did you do?" This question is what we call a Behavioral Question, which is a type of question that is much harder to practice and to fake than standard knowledge questions. People will need to come up with actual stories of things they did in the past. They cannot prepare for that by finding everything they ever did on the Internet, unless your job candidate is Kim Kardashian.

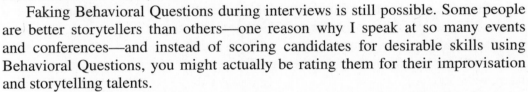

Faking Behavioral Questions during interviews is still possible. Some people are better storytellers than others—one reason why I speak at so many events and conferences—and instead of scoring candidates for desirable skills using Behavioral Questions, you might actually be rating them for their improvisation and storytelling talents.

Another issue with Behavioral Questions is that results achieved in the past offer no guarantees for the future. How a candidate behaved in an earlier job will have depended on that earlier company, with the colleagues she had at that time. It is not a reliable indication of what will happen in the future, with your company and the new team members that she could be working with soon. Don't get me wrong, though. The predictive value of Behavioral Questions is still better than that of knowledge questions and brain teasers. But times change, companies change, and people change. It's better to hire for the future than for the past.

On the company's roof terrace, in sunny Helsinki, Petri Haapio explained to me how Reaktor usually handles Job Interviews.

We have, first of all, three interview rounds with different people interviewing. The first round is where most of the candidates drop off. It typically takes one to one and a half hours and our interviewers need to assess, for example, "What if I was in an airport and the flight was delayed, and I needed to spend six hours with this person at the airport. Would that be fine or not?" Our second interview is the crucial one. There, we need to figure out what are the person's ambition level, skill level, knowledge level, and all that stuff. This second interview takes longer, typically between two and three hours. And we ask some candidates to give a short presentation on a topic that they would like to talk about or on anything else that our interviewers think is useful to assess the skills of the candidate. The third interview is basically a formality. We've made the decision already, but we still want to check if everything is okay from both sides, that we understand each other, what the compensation will be, and so on.

Petri Haapio, partner at Reaktor, Helsinki, Finland

What would you do when you needed a good cook? Would you ask job applicants for their cooking diplomas or certificates? Such information is easily faked. Would you ask them to explain to you how they usually make a spaghetti bolognese, a crème brûlée, or a Sachertorte? This would be a more reliable test than just asking for a diploma. A Behavioral Question would be like, "Tell me about the last time you made a chicken pie. What did you do? What were the complications and what were your personal improvisations to the recipe?" Or would the most effective thing be to ask something like, "Can you prepare a paella *right now*? I have everything you will need in the kitchen."

The best kind of question in Job Interviews is the Behavioral Test, which validates an actual behavior in the moment, not merely a story about that behavior in the past. When you're hiring a teacher, ask him to teach you something. When you want to test the skills of a programmer, ask her to do some actual software development. Duh. If you want your new employees to have a sense of humor, don't ask them, "Are you funny?" or "Tell me about the last time you made somebody laugh." Just don't say anything and only give the job candidate a good score when, at some point during their entire visit or interview, they made somebody laugh.

Validation of desirable behaviors through Behavioral Tests is the number one predictive factor of job performance. True heroes are defined by their actions, not their words.

Jakub Piwnik, communications manager at Brainly in Kraków, Poland, had something to say about that, too.

> *The most important part is something that we call a demo day. We actually bring the candidate here for a whole day, and they spend the day just working on a project with a team and having the opportunity to speak with their future teammates. And in between, they all have lunch together. It's a chance for us to see if this is really the person we're looking for, but also a chance to see if they relate to the culture that we have here. At the end of the demo day, there's usually a short presentation that we ask the candidate to give to the team, and then the team has an open discussion. So, people who vote to hire this person say why, and vice versa. At the end of the discussion, there's a decision. And then it's up to the candidate to accept or not. Because the demo day is also a chance for the candidate to see if this is a company that they want to contribute to.*
> *Jakub Piwnik, communications manager at Brainly in Kraków, Poland*

For many skills, Behavioral Tests are easy to create, because you can simply ask the person to do a bit of work for which those skills are needed. However, it gets tricky when it comes to attitude, values, and other qualities that you may have documented in your Culture Code. For example, how would you test if someone is open about their mistakes? In a Behavioral Test, you would have to make sure they *believe* they made a mistake during the Job Interview and then they should decide whether to be open and honest about it.

If you do your job well as a hiring manager, you find evidence for all skills, traits, and other attributes that you have listed on your Hiring Scorecard. For some of the stages in the hiring process, you involve your team so that you can share and discuss each other's perspectives and insights. This also helps you check that you have only considered the actual observable behaviors of the candidate. If you cannot back up a judgment with something the candidate said or did, then it should not be used in the evaluation.

The weeks before the big San Diego event were both difficult and exciting. Unsurprisingly, because of the loss of a team member, our Burn Chart indicated that we would be delivering less than we had hoped. I was worried about not having a product that was good enough to show up with. At the same time, we noticed that there was some uptake in usage of our platform. The first hints at gamification that we were building into the system were having some effects and there were other early signs that the product could actually work. But our team needed reinforcement. Knowing that adding people to a late project only makes it later, we had agreed to hire a new team member immediately after the deadline of Project San Diego.

During one of our Agile Retrospectives, halfway Project San Diego, we had discussed that our hiring process needed improvement. It was slow, unstructured, and too biased. So, I had spent significant time on an improved Recruitment Funnel, a new Hiring Scorecard, and better questions for the Job Interviews.

I put the new approach to the test when I had a Job Interview with a candidate who could start working with us just after the San Diego event. The evaluations on his Hiring Scorecard looked pretty good and it seemed that we had a great candidate on our hands. Near the end of the interview, I said, "You seem like a great candidate, so I hope you will pass the next round. I have here a list of the questions that our other team members are going to ask you in the next interview. Don't tell anyone, but would you like a sneak preview of those questions in advance?" The job candidate declined my offer politely and I wrote "Strong Yes" on the last empty line of the scorecard, which said, "The candidate has integrity."

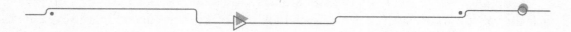

For related notes, articles, books, examples, and downloads, check out this web page: https://startup-scaleup-screwup.com/job-interviews.

The Darkest Road

Manage the expectations of stakeholders with a Product Roadmap, created with experiments, outcomes, and a Rolling-Wave Planning.

"When will there be an iOS version?"

It was probably the most frequently asked question we received when we showed our product at the big Agile2018 event in San Diego. Each time, our answer was, "We will work on iOS after we have found Product/Market Fit." As long as customers don't use our product often enough, it makes no sense to scale out to other platforms. Why duplicate something that's still not good? Clearly, our potential customers didn't see it like that. They were just eager to try our app on their favorite smartphone, which is an Android phone for some, and an iPhone for others.

Some technical readers might wonder why we didn't use a framework that could compile to Android and iOS simultaneously. The first answer is that, as a startup, what we needed most was rapid experimentation, and you can only be fast in what you're good at. Our team happened to have great Android developers. As long as we were still building Minimal Viable Products while seeking Product/Market Fit in the Validation stage, we considered it okay to use technologies in which we were fast and flexible. Switching technologies and rebuilding the base is a matter for the Stabilization stage—if or when we get there.

Our team did try to guess when would be a right time to start working on the iOS version. First, we thought it would be in the second quarter of the year. Then we communicated that it would be after the summer. Then we said it could be near the end of the year, at the earliest. No matter what we think will happen with our product development, things always change. Our plans change more often than the weather in Holland.

Creating a Product Roadmap, a high-level summary that maps out the evolution of a product toward a Product Vision, is one of the most difficult challenges for both startups and scaleups. Customers, investors, board members, and employees all require some clarity about where the company will be heading in the near future. It's a journey. People have the right to know if they want to be part of that journey. On top of that, founders want to be sure that their teams are working on the areas that have the highest business value. (I wrote that last sentence in pure agony.)

In addition to that, some stakeholders in the organization need date-based commitments or milestones from the product team for preparing marketing campaigns, training programs, or customer support. And the product team itself needs a planning for its own Recruitment Funnel and to get date-based commitments from others. Clearly, the Product Roadmap is an important instrument to communicate a product plan to all stakeholders.

At Pipedrive in Tallinn, Sergei Anikin, continued telling me about his experiences in product development as a CTO of the company.

With over 400 employees as a company and over 180 engineers in the engineering organization, we have trouble with prioritizing ideas because there are so many of them. How do you know which ones are the most important? It's good that a lot of direction is still coming from the founders. They understand the customer problem better than anyone else because they had the original Product Vision, which obviously changes over time because we get feedback from clients and the market keeps shifting and so on. But as long as the vision of the founders hasn't been realized, they still have this original roadmap in their heads. Sometimes, we have to take some steps back and maybe rebuild a few things. We have done a lot of rebuilding over time because the feedback keeps coming. The key is, it's not about a feature race. It's more about what's really

*important for the customer and what's preventing them from actually
using this tool to its full potential.*

> *Sergei Anikin, CTO at Pipedrive, Tallinn, Estonia*

It makes sense that founders keep giving direction to the Product Roadmap
with their Product Vision, but they are not the only ones with good ideas. Boris
Diebold, CTO at Seven Senders in Berlin, told me how he once collected input
when he was still working at a previous company.

> *During a company standup on Monday, I announced that I would be
> running a product strategy exercise and I wanted everyone to come
> up with product ideas and to think about where we should go with the
> product and why. I asked not only product people but the whole company
> because everyone was very engaged with our product. I said, "Hey, I
> need your help. I will be available the whole week and I will hear all your
> great ideas and then we will see how we bind it all together and make
> something out of it." I gave them a template, so they could think about
> a few questions and then they could bring me whatever they wanted. I
> talked to about 40 people in one week and there were a lot of great ideas.
> I saw some patterns among the ideas, extracted the archetypes, and
> together with the CEO, who was also one of the founders, I shaped the
> thinking further. We then discussed these refined ideas with a smaller,
> highly engaged group out of the original ones and crystallized the product
> vision from it. The whole process was highly timeboxed and took place in
> just two weeks. We found out that the best input doesn't necessarily come
> from product managers, but from hidden champions among the teams that
> had super great ideas. Also, involving everyone in the process, rather than
> running it behind closed doors, gave the team a real energy boost after
> the vision was locked in. This was very, very interesting.*
>
> *Boris Diebold, CTO at Seven Senders, Berlin, Germany*

Back in Tallinn, people experience lead Jeff McClelland told me that the
Product Roadmap planning and replanning at TransferWise is a lot of work and it
involves all teams.

One of our practices is our quarterly planning, which is quite intense.
With 1,200 people at the company, we reset our plans every quarter.
We do that because it is a communication mechanism. Teams talk with
their sister teams, the ones that operate next to them in the business, at
least once per quarter about what they are going to do next. So, there's
a lot of feedback between people in teams about their plans and they try
to agree on some commitments between the teams. Ideally, each team
is independent, but in reality, this is never really true. No team is truly
independent, so they have to coordinate their plans.
> *Jeff McClelland, people experience lead at TransferWise,*
> *Tallinn, Estonia*

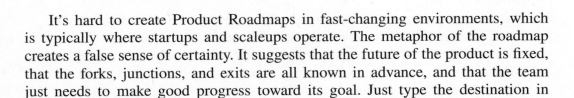

It's hard to create Product Roadmaps in fast-changing environments, which is typically where startups and scaleups operate. The metaphor of the roadmap creates a false sense of certainty. It suggests that the future of the product is fixed, that the forks, junctions, and exits are all known in advance, and that the team just needs to make good progress toward its goal. Just type the destination in Waze, turn on the hazard and traffic alerts, and off you go! But reality couldn't be more different.

For a product team, particularly in the early stages of the Business Lifecycle, the future is mostly unknown because priorities change all the time and there are many unvalidated assumptions that need testing. Making progress along a roadmap with untested hypotheses naturally leads to new insights, which leads to changed priorities, which leads to a new version of the roadmap. Planned product features and releases get postponed, or even disappear altogether, which causes disappointment among stakeholders. As a result of that, credibility and trust suffer, all because people are only doing what they're supposed to be doing: trying things to see if they work.

The solution to all of this requires three important changes to roadmap design, resulting in a Product Roadmap that shows major experiments and outcomes on a fading timeline. When you treat your roadmap as a plan of learnings and outcomes, with a forecast that gets fuzzier toward the future, you can significantly reduce the continuous disappointment among your stakeholders.

The first part of Product Roadmap redesign is to focus on experiments. The main job of startups is figuring out what works and what doesn't by running Lean Experiments. Exploration is the primary mode of operation from the Initiation stage (1) to the Stabilization stage (5). This means that, when a startup team puts something on a roadmap, rather than adding features with delivery dates, they better add experiments with learning dates.

Instead of my team promising to our customers that an iOS version will become available in a certain month, it is better first to figure out how to approach multi-platform development. We have no idea how long it takes to make an iOS version of our product unless we know first how we're going to develop across multiple devices. In other words, a better promise is to have a decision on multiplatform development by a certain date. Likewise, all other dates that you communicate to stakeholders on your roadmap should be dates by which you plan to have finished experiments and gained important insights.

The second part of Product Roadmap redesign, more relevant to scaleups than to startups, is to think in terms of business objectives and customer benefits rather than individual features. Focus on outcomes instead of output by considering what kind of results would translate to progress toward your North Star Metric. Instead of promising to deliver specific solutions consisting of features, you promise to address certain themes aiming for benefits.

For example, when you communicate a benefit such as "browsing and viewing functions usable on iPhones," you steer clear of committing to specific technological solutions. The longer you wait to communicate a specific solution, the more information you will have available to pick the best one. Some refer to this approach as a goal-oriented roadmap. The dates you communicate to stakeholders will be dates by which you plan to have solved important problems, without being specific about how you will achieve that.

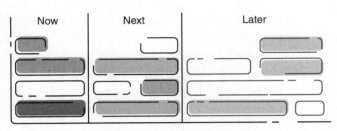

FIGURE 18.1 Rolling-Wave Planning

The third part of Product Roadmap redesign, helping you deal with the challenge of ever-changing priorities, is to apply a Rolling-Wave Planning (see Figure 18.1). You split your roadmap into several parts, often three, that you call *Now*, *Next*, and *Later*, or *Near-Term*, *Mid-Term*, and *Long-Term*. The first segment covers one to four weeks; the second is one to three months out, and the last covers everything that is at least three months away. (Your exact time frames may differ, but the principle remains the same.)

When you divide your Product Roadmap into three time frames like this, and you assign vague names such as Now–Next–Later to those time periods, rather than specific dates and months, any reader can understand that you feel pretty certain about what you're working on *now*; you are less certain about what comes *next*, and you're still very uncertain about all the experiments and outcomes planned *later*.

The team at the user experience analytics company in Paris told me that a Rolling-Wave Planning is for them basically a sweet spot between what the external stakeholders want to hear and what the development team wants to promise.

> *We ask our customers to sign up for 24 months. So, we need to find the right balance of promising product releases and adapting to change because we cannot just ask them to give us a blank check and say, "Sorry, we do not have a roadmap. It will be a surprise. Just trust us." So, we do have a three-year Product Vision that we share with our clients. And then we commit to a detailed three-month roadmap, and then we have some areas of interest for the year to come, but anything more than three months away is not a commitment.*
>
> *This is a topic of some frustration for our sales team. As long as ideas are in the three-month time frame, things are okay because they know exactly what to expect. But if the ideas are in the interest area, they don't know if they need to wait three months or nine months or even longer. But with a one-year roadmap, we would certainly be wrong, and we would deliver only 60 percent of what we had in mind. At the same time, we have*

developers who are always saying that committing to any date is the worst thing ever because estimation is a waste of time, and if you had no fixed dates at all, everything would be more agile and free and everything. But we don't live in an ideal world. We have to run a business. That's why sometimes we take developers with us to client meetings because they have to understand why it's important for sales and for clients to agree on a few delivery dates.

When you have a Rolling-Wave Planning, you can emphasize the level of uncertainty that's increasing into the future with some smart design choices. For example, you can make sure that later items on the planning are slowly fading out. You can add dates and people's names only to items in the first segment while limiting or ignoring dates and names in the other two segments. Or you can choose to use just half of the available space for your roadmap and then write "here be dragons" on the other half. Such simple tricks will further reinforce the idea that, further out, everything is too uncertain to be specific about these things.

You can easily make a Product Roadmap with a spreadsheet, a whiteboard, or some other simple visualization tool. By using the three techniques of focusing on experiments and learning, promising outcomes instead of features, and creating a Rolling-Wave Planning, you can reduce people's need for specific dates to the absolute minimum. As much as you can, in any externally facing roadmap, try not to include milestones and launch dates, unless there is a critical need to do so. (A Pitch Deck could be one of those exceptions.)

For startups, the primary goal is the validation of Product/Market Fit and Business/Market Fit, which is an exploration phase of which the results cannot simply be scheduled. It's like driving on an unknown road in the dark, without a map. For scaleups, since you already know that your business works, your goal is getting and keeping customers, and you shift from exploration and learning to execution and outcomes. But your business environment is unlikely to ever become stable and predictable. The fewer promises you make, the fewer you will have to break. As a founder, there's no need to be a politician.

The simpler you make your Product Roadmap, the smaller the chance you get stuck with stakeholder perceptions that you will need to rectify later. Try to tell a story with your Product Roadmap of how you plan to evolve the current product toward your Product Vision. Say to your stakeholders, "This is the path that we think we will be traveling. But things might change." Any work that doesn't contribute to the story, does not belong on the Product Roadmap.

When you don't tell a cohesive story with your roadmap, you leave it up to the imaginations of your customers and investors what to expect from you. Given people's often optimistic ideas about workloads, those expectations could be a lot higher than what you are capable of doing. With a Product Roadmap, you keep everyone's ideas about your progress reasonable and realistic. Don't let your stakeholders do the planning for you. Everyone sucks at making plans. It's best to make sure that any bad plans you suffer are your own.

For related notes, articles, books, examples, and downloads, check out this web page: https://startup-scaleup-screwup.com/product-roadmap.

Ghost Writer in the Sky

Set yourself up for content marketing and e-mail marketing with a Content Calendar and a Content Backlog.

"Survey of content topics"
"Hiring scorecard"
"Next team offsite"

The issues of the day appeared in the chat window during our Daily Cafe. I added that I wanted to discuss an update to our corporate website and another team member on our video call mentioned that our blog needed more articles. It seemed our team had plenty of writing to do.

I wouldn't be where I am today if I hadn't started writing. When you believe you have something meaningful to contribute to the world, you have to get your message out. This doesn't need to be in written form. It could be audio or video or any combination of formats. The details don't matter for now. You are an entrepreneur or intrapreneur and you have a few things to say. When you decide to communicate something interesting to the world, you take your first step in content marketing.

Start your content marketing earlier rather than later. The best moment is when you start thinking about your product or service, or when you created a Product Vision, in the Initiation stage (1). It takes a long time to reap the benefits of content marketing. And it's hard to keep up the discipline and produce a steady stream of content that supports your product or service and that will attract customers, employees, and business partners. Therefore, if you haven't already started, it's best to start practicing now.

In the offices of Intercom, overlooking St. Stephen's Green in Dublin, John Collins, director of content, told me all about content creation at his company.

In the early days of Intercom, no one had a marketing hat on. Nobody's job title was marketing. The big thing we had was content. Our founders were always writing. Even before Intercom became a company, they were already blogging and talking about their journey. And I'm just now sharing what they have learned. Content creation was a big thing that they were doing, and that people now talk about as part of marketing. But the founders weren't thinking about it as marketing.
John Collins, director of content at Intercom, Dublin, Ireland

In startup literature and at startup events, many business failures are blamed on bad marketing. It is not a *lack* of marketing that is the reason for the screwups; it is *poor* marketing. In my experience, what's poor about many marketing efforts is that founders and entrepreneurs are trying too hard to do marketing. They lose their authenticity because they just want to convince and convert. The better marketing campaigns, in my less-than-humble opinion, are those that try to tell a story, share an insight, or offer a useful tool. The best marketers are those who (to some extent) forget about marketing and just aim to be helpful. Potential clients and users appreciate businesses that are interesting and helpful. Content creation is an effective way to achieve that.

The only way to have success with content marketing is to publish content pieces at a regular cadence and with a consistent message. A Content Calendar (or Editorial Calendar) is often used by writers, bloggers, vloggers, podcasters, and Instagrammers to plan and manage the creation and publication of content items across different media channels, including newsletters,

blogs, and social media networks. The purpose of such a calendar is to help everyone on a team understand what is being produced and published, where, and by whom. It also ensures that the team maintains regularity and consistency of their message across multiple publications. It's no problem if the diversity in your company makes it look like the Muppet Show because, despite all the chaos, even the Muppets had regularity and consistency.

From personal experience, I know that content marketing is easier explained than performed. (I wrote the first draft of this chapter in full realization of the fact that I hadn't blogged anything new in the preceding three months. I was too busy! And here you are, reading my advice.) But when you're just winging it, and you only publish something when you're in the mood for it, you're not doing any better than gardeners who only show up to maintain a park when they want to enjoy a few hours in the sun. The result is unlikely to look pretty. So, let's put on our gloves and boots and discuss the basics of content marketing that could benefit founders and business leaders.

John Collins continued his story about content creation.

There are some people in content marketing who are now saying that, actually, less is more. You're better off publishing maybe once a week and producing something of really high quality, rather than trying to publish every day. At Intercom, we're probably somewhere in the middle. Yes, we do have a calendar. It's a very simple one. We use Trello. The calendar view in Trello is great. We have a template to make sure that all the checks and balances are in place. We created a style guide that gives people guidance on voice and tone. And when we had everything in place, we launched a podcast and wrote our first books.

John Collins, director of content at Intercom, Dublin, Ireland

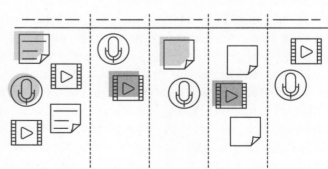

Content Calendars come in different styles. Some are actual monthly calendars showing what happens on each day of the month. Others are more loosely structured with, for example, only a column per week or a column per month, and the

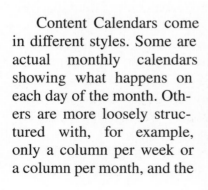

items in those columns showing cards for different content pieces. An additional option is to maintain a Content Kanban, a Kanban Board for content items that are in progress. The benefit of a Kanban Board is that it enables you to see the workflow of content items and experiment with WIP Limits. A drawback is that you can't easily see the publication schedule of those same items. The best visualization technique depends on your preference and the frequency and the amount of content that you produce.

Many content creators also maintain a Content Backlog, which is the idea list for future content items that haven't yet been assigned to specific days, weeks, or months. The Content Backlog feeds into the Content Calendar or Content Kanban. Whenever an item from the backlog gets picked up for production, it is moved onto the calendar or Kanban Board. An additional tool to maintain a backlog is not always needed. A simple version of a Content Backlog can be the first column on the calendar or on the board, with no specific date or status assigned to it. Any other place where you can easily maintain a wish list for future content items is also fine.

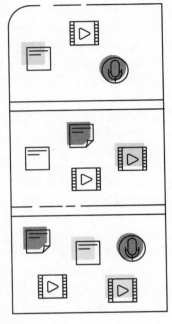

Now let's have a look at the actual content to be produced by you and your team. Obviously, you should create stuff that resonates with the users and customers that you, hopefully, described with Lean Personas. However, it's important to go wider than that and consider potential investors, employees, and business partners as consumers of your content. You might even want to create separate Lean Personas for those additional target audiences because different audiences are probably interested in different content. Therefore, each content item that you produce should have a target audience defined for it.

The Lean Persona descriptions that you create should guide you in your decisions on where to best offer your content, what types of content you should offer, and how many items you should publish per audience per month. In the beginning, you will want to pick a small set of content types to focus on. You could offer interviews, how-to guides, listicles, stories, case studies, press releases, investor updates, top tips, statistics, and much more. But you can't do it all.

Likewise, you must decide on the content channels you will use to publish and distribute your content. You could have blog posts, newsletters, podcasts, videos, social media updates, and so on. The best channels, and the optimal publication frequency, depend on your target audiences. Not surprisingly, content types and content channels are related. Infographics do well in blog posts and on social media, not so much in podcasts. White papers are great to offer on websites. In video, not really.

Next, discuss your content strategy with the team. What will make your communication stand out from the competition? How are your ideas and your style going to be remarkable? This is where you need to think about the brand that you are building and what it should mean to your stakeholders. For example, if you want to be seen as a transparent company, write blog posts about the things you learned from your failures. If you want to be recognized as a provider of quality products, create good-looking videos in which you help people improve their work-lives. Your content must reflect what your brand wants to represent.

Have an opinion. What do you actually believe that's different than other people? If you have a startup, you already believe something is different because you basically said, "We see this problem that nobody else is addressing." Or, "We see this problem. Others are attacking it that way. We're doing it this way." Very much try and create content that embodies your philosophy that you have about the world. A common mistake I see all the time these days is that big brands create a content machine with good, edgy, interesting content. But what they create has zero relevance to their main business. Make sure the content you're producing has some relationship to your products. But also, have an opinion. Think of how you're going to stand out from the crowd. There's just so much content out there that you have to try and think about what's your unique take on things.
John Collins, director of content at Intercom, Dublin, Ireland

Next up are your goals. What do you want to achieve with your content pieces? Do you want to drive attendance to online events? Do you want customers to download a trial version of your product? Do you want investors to sign up for your Equity Crowdfunding? Content items usually come with a *call to action*, and for each piece, the outcomes it is meant to realize should be clear. This could be about your North Star Metric, the Pirate Metrics, or some other goals that you have identified. Whatever it is that's important to you, if you don't measure, you have no insights into the effectiveness of your content.

Some of you may wonder where you find ideas. Personally, I think that could be the easiest part of content marketing. Just look around inside your company. You should find plenty of half-baked ideas, events, stories, and artifacts that could be input for your next blog post, video, podcast, or social media post. When team members aren't good at writing high-quality stuff themselves, just ask them for their thoughts and do the ghost writing for them. Old presentation slide decks, data from a product survey, photos from your recent team offsite, expertise and experiences of your team members, the results of your Lean Experiments, the newest version of your Culture Code or Pitch Deck, and of course, new insights about your Product Vision. They can all be dusted off, beautified, and molded into fascinating new content assets. Or you could pick a fight with the universe, and complain publicly about everything, as I do.

When you have everything in place for your content process, you can start planning your content items. Spend some time investigating the days of the year that are important to your business. Are there holidays, industry events, world events, product launches, campaigns, trade shows, or conferences, that are relevant to you and your audience? Do the start and the end of the seasons have a specific importance in any way? Are you considering World Book Day (April 23), Star Wars Day (May 4), World Emoji Day (July 17), World Animal Day (October 4), or some other festive and commemorative days, either local or global? Your Content Calendar is the place where you should mark these dates with open slots that will have to be filled with content pieces. Above all, make the right connection between the meaning of those dates and what you want your brand to stand for.

Don't forget that you have goals for your content. There are things you want your target audiences to do. Even if it's only reading what you wrote, listening to what you said, and feeling good about your brand, you still want to know whether your content marketing efforts are having an effect. Make it a habit to always check the statistics. Which content types score the best? Which channels are growing, and which are not? What do the metrics say of your calls to action? I won't try to turn you into a full-time content marketer, but everyone who produces content on a regular basis, and that includes the best founders and business leaders, needs to be aware of the return on investment. You want your Muppet Show to be a great success.

For related notes, articles, books, examples, and downloads, check out this web page: https://startup-scaleup-screwup.com/content-calendar.

Million-Dollar Gamble

Aim for Agile Funding of your business with small batches, small budgets, and keeping multiple options open.

Imagine going to a casino with a friend. Together, you decide to pool your resources because you believe that the combined efforts will increase your chances of winning big. However, your friend insists that you play exclusively on the roulette wheel and he wants to bet only on a single number because the payout, when you win, will be huge. There's just one important difference between you and your friend. For him, it's only 1/40th of his gambling budget and he plays the same game with 39 other friends at 39 other tables. For you, it's not just your entire gambling budget. It's all the money you have. Now, how do you feel about betting on a single number?

This is the feeling you should have when you take money from a venture capitalist (VC). The business model of VCs requires them to make many bets on potential unicorn companies, businesses that grow to be worth $1 billion or more. They spread their funds over lots of startups and then push all of them to be the next Spotify, Zalando, or Revolut. Anything less than that is not very interesting for them. Sadly, maybe only 1 out of 40 startups becomes such a unicorn company. Most of the others falter, wither, and die.

When you take money from venture capitalists, their agendas need to align with yours. With VCs on board, you don't have the option of saying, "I think having a company that's worth only $100 million is also nice. There's nothing wrong with betting on the odd and even numbers on the roulette wheel. The payout is smaller, but so is the risk of losing it all." That may be true, but VCs are not interested in that. They don't like small company "exits." They want unicorns. They want to go all in. With a small portion of their money, and with most of yours.

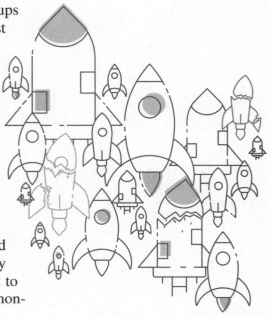

The founders of several VC-funded businesses told me that, if they had to do it all over, they probably wouldn't take money from VCs. Once you take them on board, and let them pay for your gas, you will be traveling together. If you don't steer in their preferred direction, in rare cases, they might even take over the wheel and throw you out of the bus. It is important to understand that it's easier to divorce from your spouse than it is to throw out an investor.

I'm writing this chapter while we are preparing our next round of funding. I had six meetings with investors today. Two venture capitalists and four angel investors. To be honest, I don't really favor the VC approach. I prefer to keep my options open for as long as I can. VC-backed startups tend to grab all the headlines, but the success of a business should not be measured by how many articles appear in the media, and how much VC-money was poured into the business. There is nothing wrong with alternatively funded companies, many of which operate mostly under the radar. Fortunately, there are quite a few alternative options available for startups besides venture capital. And that's great because raising capital is a project in itself and many startups have screwed up because they ran out of cash and wisdom before they ran out of ideas and experiments.

Kristjan Koik, the CEO of Flender in Dublin, told me about such earlier screwups.

We haven't made a big mistake with Flender yet because we've learned from the screwups with our previous startups. They were fantastic startups, with big customers, but we didn't attract enough investment at the right time. We lost our momentum because of that. And then we ran out of money.

Kristjan Koik, CEO of Flender, Dublin, Ireland

Daniel Krauss, cofounder and CIO at FlixBus, was having a few drinks with me at a terrace in Berlin, Germany. He told me various fascinating details about the funding process.

Funding is still one of the non-agile parts of the startup environment, which is obvious because the concept comes from the stock market. Some people think they get a better return on their investments when they do closed investment rounds. But still, the rhythm of the business is orders, annuals, closings, and everything. And then they have their limited partners who usually put money into funds that run 10 years. All those financing cycles are not very agile. And you suffer from that as a company because they require you to come up with annual budgets and things like that.

Daniel Krauss, cofounder and CIO at FlixBus, Berlin, Germany

It's important to recognize that what gets funded is usually a business model. Teams and projects cannot generate a return on investment, but a business model can. The funding of business models often takes place in stages that, roughly, correspond to the Shiftup Business Lifecycle. Only a small amount of time is needed to produce a Product Vision in the Initiation stage (1). A bit more effort is needed to enable the exploration of Problem/Solution Fit in the Expedition stage (2). Somewhat bigger wallets are needed for Formation (3), and then for the ongoing support of the Product/Market Fit search in Validation (4) and Business/Market Fit in Stabilization (5). And finally, very big wallets will have to be pulled open when it ever comes to Acceleration (6).

For the funding of a new business, it doesn't make much difference whether we're talking about an independent startup or a corporate startup. Both need budgets for the development of ideas, prototypes, and beta versions. Both need to show progress and build trust in order to get more funds later. And there shouldn't be much difference between an independent investor and a corporate portfolio manager, either. Both should feed startups with funds that are just small enough to cover the activities in the next stage. Both should insist that the funds are used to get to the next milestone and to seek evidence of a profitable future to make additional funds negotiable.

It is typical for independent startups to seek funding for financial runways of 12 to 18 months. This means that, every year to year-and-a-half, a significant amount of a founder's time and attention goes into finding money to cover the next stage of the Business Lifecycle, or at least a significant part of that. This easily costs them most of their time, for several weeks or months in a row, with dozens of investor meetings full of plans, presentations, and performances. Once they have completed the round and acquired the funds, the founders can focus on spending the money and working toward the next milestone, until the whole circus starts again a year later. It's like the annual Eurovision Song Contest, but with a more critical jury and less colorful outfits.

Daniel Krauss of FlixBus continued his story about the funding process.

I think managing investors through the entire process takes probably half a year. If you want to do that seriously, with good preparations, and with a good valuation at the end, it takes one person, full-time. We were three founders, so we could share the burden. But funding is a full-time job, and it's a founder's job, in my point of view. This is one of the reasons why you really should try to build a good team as early as you can because then the team can tackle all the product stuff while you focus on getting the business funded.

     Daniel Krauss, cofounder and CIO at FlixBus, Berlin, Germany

Kristjan Koik of Flender gave me his perspective on it.

We just closed an equity finance challenge from an early stage VC. This was another milestone because all the previous investments were private individuals. This was probably a six- to eight-month process. For the CEO and the chairman, a lot of effort goes there. I would say, it's a lot harder for early-stage companies, for two specific reasons. First, the company is doing this kind of funding for the first time, and there are a lot of things to prove to investors. But also, when you're still in an early stage, you probably don't have a massive team. When you're doing your second or third round, you probably have a fully built team that you can delegate stuff to while you're doing the fundraising. Whereas in the early stage, that's a full-time job.

Kristjan Koik, CEO of Flender, Dublin, Ireland

When a lot of time goes into planning and preparations, just to get a project funded, experts in business agility sometimes refer to that as Big Design Up Front (BDUF). An important reason for these long funding runways is that the investment process is costly and painful because of the meetings, negotiations, due diligence, and legal fees. But agilists like to say, "When something hurts, do it more often." When you force yourself to be creative and make everything less costly and less painful, and by breaking up your funding rounds into shorter increments, you can move toward many small rounds of funding or, as I like to call it, *Agile Funding*. With a bit of research and preparation, you could Always Be Funding (ABF).

Fortunately, the concept of business agility is taking over the startup world. Funding runways are getting shorter. With the emergence of Equity Crowdfunding platforms, getting money has become so much easier that some startups raise capital four, five, or six times, in small increments. To me, this makes a lot of sense. Why offer investors forecasts and milestones that extend two years into the future? Everyone knows such predictions are meaningless in a rapidly evolving environment. By raising money more often, in smaller rounds, founders can set more realistic, short-term goals, focus on achieving those milestones, and build trust and credibility among investors, thereby increasing the chance that they also complete the follow-up rounds successfully. Hitting several targets after each other builds a better reputation than aiming for, and possibly missing, just one goal that's quite far away.

As a startup founder, you might want to consider getting as close as possible to the logical extreme: Continuous Funding. When something still hurts in small increments, do it even more often! Reorganize your systems so that anyone can invest in your company, at any time, from anywhere. If developers can get rid of painful software release cycles to achieve what they call continuous deployment, founders should be able to throw out their painfully slow investment rounds and aim for continuous funding. Release shares and get funds at the click of a button!

A consequence of small funding rounds is that it means you must learn to work with small budgets. When you have little money, you need ways to build less and work faster. There's no better way to push for a lean-agile approach than to be underfunded and overinspired. As many creatives know, extra constraints often lead to more innovation. Performance comes from moderation, not gluttony. It might be hard to see this as a benefit now, but I'm sure you'll thank me later.

Another way to be more agile in your funding approach is to keep multiple options open. At every stage of a startup's life, there are different ways to get funded. The longer you can postpone a commitment to one single source of funding, the more flexible you remain as a business. That means, for example, postponing the VC route for as long as you can. You can try Equity Crowdfunding once and then never look back if it didn't work out. You can work with angel investors and then go in another direction when that's better for the business. But once you start working with formal investors, there's no going back from this 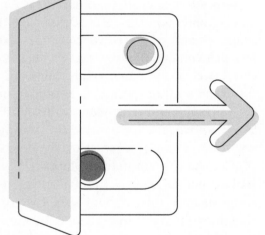 path. This means thinking ahead and doing some scenario planning. What are your options for the next stage? Which multiple approaches can you initiate in parallel to see the ones that work best for you?

My team experienced the benefits of multiple approaches when our Equity Crowdfunding was over. Originally, the crowdfunding platform that we used had told us it would take three weeks, on average, from closing the round to receiving the cash. For multiple reasons that I won't go into now (but that left me with scratch marks on the walls), the time between the end of our crowdfunding and receiving our funds turned out to be three months, not three weeks. Fortunately, besides the crowdfunding platform (for European investors), we also had our do-it-yourself crowdfunding (for non-European investors). The two approaches ran in parallel. Everyone who invested in us from outside of Europe was paying us directly, so we had enough cash coming in. If we had relied on only the crowdfunding platform, we might not have survived the successful funding. We would have reached the finish line as a corpse. Lesson learned: never depend on just one option!

Using multiple approaches has become easier because the number of options for funding has increased significantly. Twenty years ago, as a first-time entrepreneur, I could choose between rich friends, venture capitalists, and badly secured bank vaults. Nowadays, there are incubators, accelerators, angels, grants, crowdfunding, peer-to-peer lending, initial coin offerings (ICOs), and the list goes on. When the number of possibilities to solve a problem increases, smart people try multiple approaches to see which option gives them the best return, with the least effort.

Let's have a quick look at the popular options.

I financed the first stages of my current business myself. The company was *self-funded*. I had my income from speeches, book writing, and courseware licensing, which was enough to cover the initial costs. Other entrepreneurs pay for their early business ideas in a similar way through freelancing, employment, or running another business model in parallel. Financing business A with the income from business B is just another way of keeping your options open.

Another possibility is to get people from your personal network to fund your business. Some call this the category of *friends, family, and fools*. (No, this is not Dutch bluntness. It is an often-used expression in the startup world.) This is about people with small wallets that, most likely, you already knew before you started your business. But please, take care that your friendships won't tank when your business does.

Closely related is the category of *angel investors*. These are people with larger wallets who are interested in your business because informal investing is their hobby. Most likely, you have not been in personal contact with them and it's easiest to get to know them through startup events or personal connections. Angel investors bring knowledge and extensive experience to the table, but finding such investors requires a significant effort in informal networking.

When your business model allows it, you could try and aim for *customer funding*. The healthiest form of funding is when revenues from clients are enough to sustain your business. You could consider pre-orders of new products, down payments for batched work, or annual subscriptions that customers pay for at the start of a year. The earlier you get clients to pay for your business, the better.

Another term that you may come across is *bootstrapping*, which is not really a separate option because it is commonly understood as a combination of self-funding and customer funding. Pay for your own business until you get customers to do it for you. Some experts claim that bootstrapping is the best of all approaches, if the chosen business model allows you to do that.

At Taxify in Tallinn, Riina Einberg gave me her perspective on bootstrapping and funding.

I've been in a position where we were completely dependent on investments. In such a case, scaling is very complex and nerve-wracking. If you're able to make enough money to cover your costs, you have much more freedom and flexibility, and confidence as well because you are not so much dependent on investors, and usually your cap table and valuation are in much better shape, as well. I would say scaling without a solid business model and not making enough money is very risky. You would have to have something very attractive, something very unique, something very appealing. If you don't make money and you are just focused on limited markets, you are in a very dangerous situation.

Riina Einberg, general manager at Taxify, Tallinn, Estonia

You have already discovered that one of my favorite funding approaches is *equity crowdfunding*. Instead of selling big chunks of equity to a small number of investors, you sell small chunks of equity to a large number of investors. For an overview of the (many) benefits and (few) drawbacks, I simply refer to Chapter 6.

Closely similar to equity crowdfunding are the options of *product crowdfunding* and *initial coin offerings* (ICOs). The first involves platforms such as Kickstarter and Indiegogo and the second involves cryptocurrencies and blockchains. In both cases, you don't sell ownership of the business to the crowd but rather a certain right or privilege, such as special versions of your product or early access to your service in the future.

Some entrepreneurs like the idea of government funding through *grants* because subsidies are considered *free money*. However, the *free* subsidies offered by the state often involve a large amount of bureaucracy, with only a small chance of being offered a grant. You must be willing to do all the paperwork for the formal application procedures and, when a grant is actually offered to you, handle even more paperwork afterward to justify how you spend the money.

A possibility not frequently discussed in the mainstream media is that of *corporate funding*. Traditionally, established companies invest in new products and services with feasibility studies, big budgets, extensive business cases, and long-term plans. But they would benefit from a more lean-agile approach where they support both internal and external startups with portfolio management, stage-by-stage funding, and an innovation funnel. As a startup, you can benefit from corporations that seek to modernize their approach to innovation.

Another interesting category is that of the *incubators* and *accelerators*. These are organizations that specialize in helping startups to get from one stage to the next, in exchange for a chunk of equity, often throwing additional services into the mix, such as shared facilities, a network of advisors, and a local community of founders.

Matt Ellsworth, partner at 500 Startups, joined me over a Skype call to explain how the accelerator business works.

> *It's the community and camaraderie where global investors invest in a lot of companies from outside the U.S. When they come to San Francisco for our in-residence program, they get to meet entrepreneurs from all over the world, which is extremely helpful, because startups can be a bit unhealthy in terms of the stress and the work and everything. So, it helps to build a professional network. Some of these professionals come from places where the startup scene is really small. So, when they come to a program that has 30 to 50 companies in that same batch of people, they're able to create a huge community and network. And when you're a group of founders that are going through similar challenges, and you're meeting each week to share your progress and all those other aspects of community, I'd say those are the key things that accelerators provide.*
>
> *Matt Ellsworth, partner at 500 Startups, Paris, France*

And then there is the option of *venture capital*. The goal of formal investors is to achieve an outstanding return on their investment by only funding companies that have a good chance of scaling big. This means they are primarily interested in business models in the Stabilization stage (5) or the Acceleration stage (6), after those startups have found Business/Market Fit. Venture capitalists aim for a big exit, which requires them to push hard for rapid growth. When given a choice between a 10 percent chance of growing a $1B company versus a 50 percent chance of getting a $200M company, they will always choose the former.

Matt Elsworth from 500 Startups continued his story.

If you're going to engage in venture capital, you should have an understanding of what the person you're in business with is expecting and valuing. VCs are always going to value the potential for giant startups that make huge returns. And that's never going to change. They might like you personally and whatever, but that's their job. That's what they're there to do, which is why more companies should be smart about whether or not they actually go raise venture capital.

Matt Ellsworth, partner at 500 Startups, Paris, France

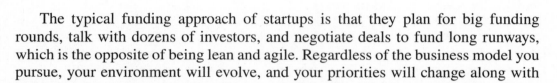

The typical funding approach of startups is that they plan for big funding rounds, talk with dozens of investors, and negotiate deals to fund long runways, which is the opposite of being lean and agile. Regardless of the business model you pursue, your environment will evolve, and your priorities will change along with it. It's smarter to set yourself up for a way of funding that can easily adapt to new situations. It can help you tremendously if you pursue an Agile Funding approach, in small stages, with small budgets, and keeping multiple options open.

The industry's romanticism of raising money is kind of like when you graduate from high school, and then you go to college, and then you need to get a salaried job, and then you need to get married, and once you're married, you have kids. There are all these life milestones and expectations that are placed on us every step of the way. The same things happen in the startup world where founders raise money and then they're expected to hire people and just run, run, run, super, super fast. And when you're only blindly doing that, you ignore market timing and all the other complex things that happen in a startup.

In the ideal situation, you raise from investors with realistic expectations, and you're honest and open with them about the process and how you're building your company. They're signing on to be on board with that and they give you support and advice along the way. And when things get rough or something doesn't go as planned, there's an open dialogue. Nobody is being kept in the dark. But I think that more people should pay attention to how fast they're growing, and I think investors should sometimes allow exceptions to the month-over-month growth rules that we have, that we've been taught to look for. It's hard to take the time to look at each company individually and to consider all the different exceptions. We see patterns. It's easy to follow those patterns even when maybe they don't apply.

Matt Ellsworth, partner at 500 Startups, Paris, France

For related notes, articles, books, examples, and downloads, check out this web page: https://startup-scaleup-screwup.com/agile-funding.

Spheres of Influence

Get insights into the creation of a Pitch Deck and learn about the essential and the optional slides.

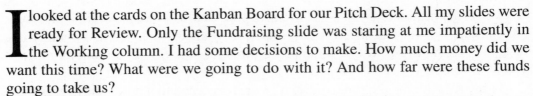

I looked at the cards on the Kanban Board for our Pitch Deck. All my slides were ready for Review. Only the Fundraising slide was staring at me impatiently in the Working column. I had some decisions to make. How much money did we want this time? What were we going to do with it? And how far were these funds going to take us?

We had a few months left before we would run out of funds and dozens of questions were still unresolved in my mind. The meetings I had with a few investors the week before only added more questions to the list. Was our burn rate really too high? Did we indeed need a narrower focus? Which funding options were we going to use at which point? And when would we finally switch from business exploration to business execution? I needed to have some answers soon because many screwups of young companies can be attributed to financial troubles, such as a lack of funds, a lack of cash flow, and a lack of interest among investors.

Many entrepreneurs and founders raise money for their businesses. Whether it's for starting up or scaling up, it is common for young companies to try and get funded. This requires expanding their spheres of influence, convincing other people to part with their money by showing them a significant return on their investment with only a small amount of risk. In the case of angel investors and formal investors, the pitch needs to be offered verbally, but investors like having something to look at, to browse through, and to discuss with their colleagues. In the case of Equity Crowdfunding, the crowd will want the same. That's why we make a Pitch Deck.

The average Pitch Deck is between 10 and 20 slides and it often comes in two versions: a readable one and a presentable one. The readable version needs to have all essential information about your company and your investment proposal so that it can be understood and discussed by investors without you being in the room. It is the one you can send to people, show on your website, or strategically leave behind at a high-society party.

The presentation version of the Pitch Deck is the one you use when you pitch your business in person and when you are there to answer any questions. It can be based on the readable version but then with many details removed from the slides and replaced with just a few relevant keywords. The reason you trim it down is so that investors look at you, and listen to you, rather than try and read your slides while you're talking. You can give them the readable version later.

Besides the split in a readable and a presentable version, it is crucial that you spend some time on a decent-looking design. Why would investors believe that you will take good care of their money when you don't take good care of your Pitch Deck? At the minimum, you want to make sure that the visuals, colors, and fonts are consistent with your logo, your product, or your website. There are many fine designers in the world who will happily do this for you. Some of them might send you an invoice.

In my research on the topic of Pitch Decks, I learned that everyone agrees there are two categories of slides: the essential ones and the optional ones. I also learned that everyone disagrees on which slides belong to which category. The division I made in this chapter is simply the result of averaging the opinions from a jury of a few dozen experts.

When you are working on a new Pitch Deck, I advise you to include all essential slides mentioned here unless you have a good reason for leaving some out. And I suggest that you skip all the optional slides unless you have a good reason for squeezing a few in. It will not surprise you that many of the slides correspond with pieces of the Business Quilt. After all, the quilt is a visualization of your business model, which is exactly the thing investors want to understand.

So, let's have a brief look at each individual slide.

With the **Cover** slide of your Pitch Deck, you need to grab people's attention and give them an idea of what to expect. Describe what your startup does with one simple tagline, preferably indicating the benefit you offer to your customers. A good picture will certainly help, and a logo has never hurt anyone.

Your **Overview** slide should explain the opportunity and the risk. In a verbal pitch, it can happen that you have time to show only one slide. Within seconds, investors want to know if your startup is the kind of business they would like to invest in (good opportunity). And they also want to know about validation, traction, and achievements (low risk).

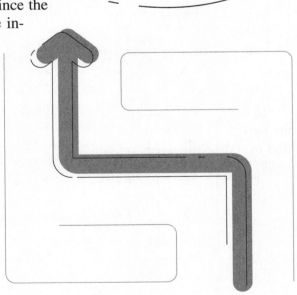

On the **Problem** slide (sometimes called *opportunity*), you explain what issue needs solving and why. You identify the people who are faced with this problem, you explain their Jobs to Be Done, and you convince the readers that the current solutions are inadequate. Offer some evidence to back up your claim that this is an opportunity worth pursuing.

What kind of **Solution** do you have and what are you doing about the problem? Do you have an app, a website, a platform, a service, or a physical product? What does it do? How does the solution achieve the benefits that will address the needs of your customers? Show the basics of your solution and let your readers realize that it could work and that it would be awesome.

On the **Customer/Target Market** slide, show that you understand who your customers are. Do you have evidence that many people would be interested in your solution? Indicate the Total Addressable Market (TAM), Serviceable Addressable Market (SAM), Serviceable Obtainable Market (SOM), and Launch Addressable Market (LAM). Use your favorite search engine to learn about these terms.

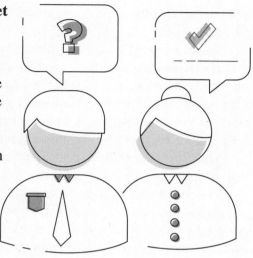

Peter Dowds, CEO and cofounder at Elder, joined me on a Skype call from London, to talk about his experiences as a startup founder in the healthcare industry.

> We decided early on that we wanted to focus on a particular problem, which is full-time care—when the need is so acute that someone needs round-the-clock support. We felt that's the area where the current solutions are the worst, and we thought that finding a niche and focusing on that niche rather than trying to boil the ocean and do everything with a broad marketplace was the most sensible approach. And that's worked really well for us. Our go-to-market strategy is tailored to this specific niche rather than a much broader attempt where you're not as sure of the problem, or you don't understand your customer as well, so you try to solve everything. This tends to be a bad idea. For us, we are focused only on people who need full-time care. There are obviously millions of people who need care, and they could be wrapped up into a broad problem, but they would need only a bit of help. Maybe one visit per day or per week. But we decided to double down, not on everyone, but on those where support is needed full-time, because there is a more acute problem there. It allowed us to differentiate ourselves.
>
> Peter Dowds, CEO and cofounder at Elder, London, United Kingdom

On the **Go-to-market Strategy** slide, you describe the customers you will reach out to first and how you are planning to get to them. Elaborate on your marketing objectives and how you are going to measure them. You can also clarify your positioning statement, what messaging you have in mind for new users, and what channels you intend to use.

The **Product** slide (sometimes referred to as the *secret sauce*) is where you explain the underlying magic of your solution. Show how your product works in a few simple steps. Use screenshots or video to reveal what happens when people use your product and how they will enjoy its benefits. A magic wand is optional.

One of the most important slides in your Pitch Deck is the one where you show **Traction**. What evidence do you have so far that indicates you are on the right path? Can you show intensive usage and high retention of early clients? Explain what you've learned from your Minimum Viable Products, or show the revenue and customers you've already acquired. Letters of intent from strong prospects will also be appreciated. For many investors, evidence of traction is the main driver for funding.

Nick Bortot, CEO and founder at BUX in Amsterdam, had his own experiences to share with me about funding.

Our product is quite volatile when you look at our revenues. We're dependent on what happens on the financial markets, so it can happen that our revenues double in a few months but then also fall back again to earlier levels. And most investors like steady, growing revenues. So sometimes, we have a slightly difficult case with investors. If you want my advice, it would

*be to knock on a lot of investors' doors. But if you don't see a sparkle
in their eyes, then it doesn't make sense to try and convince them. They
should basically love your product.*

Nick Bortot, CEO and founder at BUX, Amsterdam, The Netherlands

On the **Revenue Model** slide, you explain the
type of business model you have, what the pricing model is, the cost of production, and how
the company will turn that into profit. Important
numbers investors will want to know about are
your Customer Acquisition Costs and the Customer Lifetime Value. Yes, go ahead. Google
that. I'll wait.

The **Financials** slide could be the one that investors will scrutinize most. Show forecasts of primary
revenues and expenses for the next 12 to 24 months. The
rough estimates will be wrong but they will show that
you understand the financial hypotheses that will
need to be validated. You may want to consider
delivering three different forecasts: the optimal
scenario, your best guess, and the worst case.

In Berlin, Daniel Krauss of FlixBus offered
his opinion on the budgeting and forecasting plans
that investors are always asking for:

*Every plan and budget give a feeling of
safety and security to people, even though it's
only fake. Everybody knows that. A plan is outdated the moment it is
published, but still it's something that people can refer to. So it offers
a feeling of safety and security, which they like. And that's also one of
the challenges you have as an agile company in a scaled environment.
Agile means, to me, continuous change and iteration. In the past,
change management was always to unfreeze, do something, and then
freeze. But agile means you're continuously unstable, and that means,
to some people, that there's continuous uncertainty. And uncertainty*

feels awkward to them. Small and fast iterations are still poison for the public market and the kinds of investors who are relevant for funding. They still rely on their plans and budgets, while all investors, especially startup investors, know that every budget that they have seen over the past 10 years was BS.

Daniel Krauss, cofounder and CIO at FlixBus, Berlin, Germany

You should have a **Competition** slide because every business has some form of competition. Even if you don't have direct competitors with similar products or services, your customers will have alternatives to getting their jobs done. Show your potential investors that you understand what the competitive landscape looks like.

Explain what makes your **Team** the right one to address this opportunity. Do you have a track record of working together? You will want to show a complementary skill set and some experience in the market, the startup scene, or the technologies that you are using. Include founders, key team members, and others who are crucial to the business.

On the **Fundraising** slide (sometimes called the *ask* or *use of funds*), you will have to show how much funding you need, for how long, and why. What are you planning to do with the money? Come up with a couple of milestones that you believe you will be able to reach with the requested capital. Set yourself some targets that you feel you will be able to achieve.

On the **Conclusion** slide, you can sum it all up. It has a similar function as the overview slide at the beginning but it can be good to begin and end with a consistent message phrased in different ways: Why is this a great opportunity and how are the main risks being addressed? Oh, and don't forget your call to action: Are your contact details on the slide deck?

Apart from the essential slides, there are some optional slides that you can consider. You need to weigh the additional value of these slides against the risk of making the presentation too large. Only add one or two slides when they really add something to your story. It is easy to fall into the typical trap of reviewers. In my experience, reviewers always say, "add this," "insert that," "explain this," "clarify that," "give an example of this," and "offer a summary of that." And then they end their feedback with, "Make it smaller; it's too big."

The **Unique Value Proposition** slide corresponds with the Unique Value Proposition piece of your Business Quilt. What makes you different from the competition? Why would people buy from you rather than from someone else?

On the **Why Now** slide, you can elaborate on the timing of your product. Investors like to know that your business is not too early and not too late coming to the market. Explain why the market is ripe enough, and the trends that are converging to make this is a perfect time for your business.

A **Product Roadmap** slide can be useful, too. Some investors will want to know what's happening next. It can be good to offer your audience a Product Roadmap overview with a timeline of your priorities and upcoming releases, but without commitment on specific deadlines.

With a **Strategic Partnerships** slide, you can show the other companies that will help you reach a wider audience, get more customers, increase your revenues, and lower your expenses. Explain to your readers how you are building out your network.

Finally, it can be worth describing your **Competitive Advantage**. What makes your business model hard to copy by competitors? Are you in a position to defend your business with intellectual property, celebrity status, a large client network, or some patents?

Creating a Pitch Deck is not something you do on a Tuesday afternoon. There are only 10 to 20 slides to make but they need a lot of thought and plenty of tweaking. It is worth searching online for Pitch Deck examples of other startups. Create your readable slide deck first, find (and pay) someone to make it look awesome, and then make the presentable version by deleting everything you intend to say, rather than show, during a live presentation.

Once you've created a new Pitch Deck, it might be worth keeping it updated on a continuous basis. You may be raising funds multiple times, and it's good to always have an up-to-date slide deck on your website for new investors who express interest before the start of your next funding round. This will be even more relevant when you move toward Agile Funding, with more rounds and shorter runways.

One of the main challenges as a founder in the Validation (4) stage is that investors and customers all want to know when you're going to shift to Stabilization (5) and even Acceleration (6). People seem not to realize that the Validation stage is all about a search for a valid business model. You cannot simply set a finish time on the positive outcome of a search effort, as everyone knows who has ever lost their bank cards, their passport, or their newly purchased smartphone. (I tick all the boxes you can imagine.)

When you're pitching a business that's still in search mode, your Pitch Deck must show that you have a disciplined approach to your exploration process. It should also make it believable that, when you finally find something that works, you will have a disciplined approach to executing it. Those are two different things and they need to be explained accordingly. And all of that in just 10 to 20 slides. Good luck with that. I need plenty of it myself, as well, because I still haven't finished our Pitch Deck. It just needs a little more tweaking of the Fundraising slide.

For related notes, articles, books, examples, and downloads, check out this web page: https://startup-scaleup-screwup.com/pitch-deck.

Heart Journey

Describe the optimal customer journey and user experience with a Journey Map and discover the Moments of Truth.

The e-mail to me said, "It's been a month since the last update to your shareholders. Click here to go to your account and then choose Add Update."

I clicked on the link in the message to arrive on the crowdfunding platform, but I didn't see any button that said, "Add Update." I checked all the menus and I performed a search on the web page. There was no Add Update anywhere. Slightly frustrated, I clicked on the Help link, which launched the online support.

"How can I help?" something invisible asked me.

I answered, "I received an e-mail from you reminding me to send an update to my investors. Your e-mail says Add Update, but when I click on the link, I cannot find this feature anywhere on the website."

"Okay," the reply said, "If you want to read updates from a crowdfunding campaign, you must go to the My Investments page."

"No *&^%#, I don't want to *read* updates. I want to *add* an update. I am not an investor, I am a startup founder."

There was no further reply from online help. My profanity had probably shocked the bot. One hour later, I received an e-mail asking me to rate my satisfaction with online support on a scale of 1 to 10, and I thought to myself, "WTF?"

Customers can be annoyingly demanding. They want their experiences with your products and services to be flawless and seamless, across all mediums. They want you to understand who they are, so they don't have to repeat everything twice, but at the same time they want you to maintain high levels of privacy and security across different tools and devices. They want their experiences to be similar on different platforms, but they also want you to make use of the unique benefits of each. They want you to use the newest communication channels, but they don't want you to give up on the traditional ones too soon. Customers can be as taxing as family sometimes.

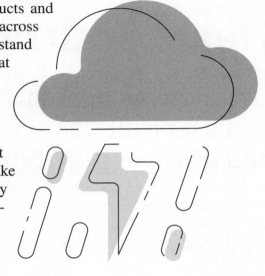

All these customer requirements get increasingly more difficult as the number of channels, platforms, devices, and tools keeps growing. Your interactions with the client might flow from an app to an instant messenger, via a website and a chatbot, to a shop and a call center. Good luck keeping that all organized!

Peter Dowds, the CEO of Elder, told me about customer experience in health care.

We are in the care sector where the stakes are very high. You can't put people at risk in the same way that you might in other industries. There's a big difference between a pizza not turning up and a carer not showing up. We recognized that early on in our approach. It all comes back to knowing your customer. One area that has really helped us is that we have an exhaustive focus on customer insight. We have developed a really deep, holistic understanding of the customer problem—exactly what our customer experience is and how that care journey develops—from doing hundreds of hours of customer interviews, and time spent with customers to really understand the nuts and bolts of what happens with them.

Peter Dowds, CEO and cofounder at Elder, London, United Kingdom

The Journey Map is a technique that helps you understand and manage the experiences of people. A Customer Journey Map (or User Journey Map, depending on the kind of persona) is a diagram that illustrates the typical levels a customer (or user) goes through while engaging with your product or service. The goal of this technique is to get a deeper understanding of what people experience. A crucial aspect of Journey Maps (sometimes referred to as *service maps* or *experience maps*) is that they always tell the story from the customer's or user's perspective. What is the next level that *they* want to achieve? It is the perfect tool to use in the Empathize and Synthesize areas of the Innovation Vortex.

Like all stories, Journey Maps are linearized presentations of nonlinear experiences. Very few customers follow a simple sequence of *steps* in their interaction with your business. Similar to games where players interact in nonlinear ways with the games and with each other, but still aim to achieve and complete a number of distinct game levels, I prefer to say that a user's engagement with you and your product evolves through different stages or levels. They are allowed to go in many different directions but, ultimately, they should be going up.

Our team has spent countless hours discussing and understanding our two primary Lean Personas, Alberto the external consultant, and Patricia the internal coach, using the input that we obtained through many customer interviews and site visits. As a collaborative effort that took several meetings, we created a high-level Journey Map to describe what would be an ideal experience for our users (see Figure 22.1).

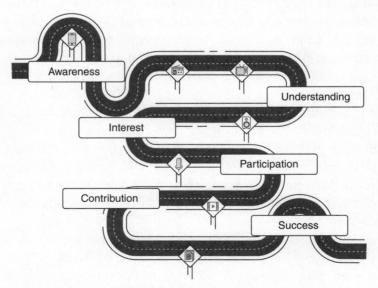

FIGURE 22.1   A High-level Journey Map

The first thing our potential clients would like is an *awareness* that our product exists, which might happen through ads, social media, blog posts, talks at events, and other channels. The next level is that they want a decent *understanding* of what our product can do for them so that they can decide if it's worth investigating further. Third, after understanding the benefits, they might want to express *interest* by signing up for our mailing list, following our social accounts, or joining our community on Slack. With enough interest, there could be a desire for *participation* by downloading our app and starting a one-month trial period. After doing this, the client will want to experience that our product provides great value so that they move on to the *contribution* phase where they not only pay for the product but also add more value to our platform. Finally, the last level is where the client confirms *success* because all needs and desires have been met. The result is a high-level Journey Map consisting of six levels or stages.

A Journey Map provides a single cross-functional view of the customer and user experience, which is the result of all outward-facing functions of your business. The tool ensures that the customer or user stays front and center in the minds of designers, developers, copywriters, marketers, and managers. Your whole team needs a common understanding of the entire journey and the needs and desires that must be satisfied along the way.

Journey Maps help your organization to achieve cohesion across many client interactions and they force your business to adapt when things go wrong halfway through a journey. With a Journey Map, it is easier to see where there's work to be done to improve people's engagement with your business. There is possibly no better tool that breaks down internal silos, forces your team members to look beyond their own responsibilities, and gets them to strive for a streamlined experience.

Developing a Journey Map often takes a number of iterations. You start with some initial hypotheses about a desirable experience for your clients. Then, over time, through many interviews and data analysis, you evolve the map into a more accurate depiction of what's really happening with people. The biggest mistake that businesses make is not investigating and validating the actual journeys that are happening with their clients. When your service makes a customer want to strangle a kitten, it is something that you need to know.

When you find out that your customers or users experience something that they didn't expect, you have identified a Moment of Truth. These are pivotal moments on your Journey Map. They are the points at which people either

say, "Holy cow, that's amazing. This is the best thing ever!" or "Oh, for God's sake, really? Please hand me a f***ing kitten." The first variant is called a *WOW* moment. I suggest we call the other one a *WTF* moment. Getting rid of all WTF moments, and optimizing the number of WOW moments, is the main goal for your team in their Journey Mapping exercises. Save a lot of kittens and find the holy cows.

> *A big thing that we're always thinking about is how we help customers to see the value of Intercom as quickly as possible. That's something we definitely talk about a lot because Intercom helps you onboard and get your users engaged with your products. So, we write about that a lot because we hope to get people to use Intercom to do that. But we also think about it a lot ourselves in terms of how we are going to get people from visiting us to being successful with our products. If there was something I would point to, throughout the history of Intercom, that has always been our focus. I'd say it's figuring out how to show value to customers as early on as possible.*
>
> *John Collins, director of content at Intercom, Dublin, Ireland*

There is no single best way to draw a Journey Map. There are many colorful variations of graphs, flow charts, tables, infographics, and storyboards that teams have produced to visualize customer and user journeys. You have a great deal of freedom to be creative and you should use the form that best communicates the story for clients and your product or service.

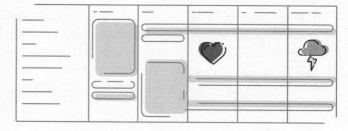

Many people draw Journey Maps as pipelines, from left to right, which might exaggerate the linearity of the experience. Perhaps, it could be better to draw them as pyramids, from bottom to top, emphasizing the nonlinearity of the experiences (horizontally), but also showing the expected progress (vertically) through different stages of engagement.

Step 1 of a Journey Mapping exercise is usually to **pick a persona**. If your team works with different Lean Personas, you may need to create different Journey Maps for each of them. Some personas could be users while others could be customers, which explains why the same practice is referred to as both user journey maps and customer journey maps in other literature. However, nothing should prevent you from making Journey Maps for patients, members, employees, donors, and other stakeholders of your business. With a new round of Equity Crowdfunding around the corner, our team has just finished making a Journey Map for crowd investors.

Step 2 is to **pick the level and focus** of your Journey Map. You can design a high-level map that visualizes the main experiences from an initial contact to the end of a contract (sometimes called *cradle to grave*). You can also choose to create low-level Journey Maps for more specific needs, such as asking a question or extending a membership. You can pick one part of your Value Proposition Wheel and draw a Journey Map to explore how clients enjoy that specific value. For example, placing and receiving one order from a web shop, renting and returning a vehicle with an app, or (dare I mention it?) sending an update to investors through a crowdfunding website.

The third step is to **define the stages**. What are the levels from the first identification of a need to a completed, satisfactory experience? It is best to keep the journey simple and to describe it as a linear story with an idealized path across different stages of the experience. For example, *Browse—Compare—Order—Wait—Receive* in the case of a purchase from a web shop, or *Enter—Engage—* *Order—Drink—Exit* in the case of a visit to a coffee bar. It is easy to get drawn into discussions about alternative paths, such as, "What if the customer makes multiple orders?" or "What happens when they need to use the restroom?" But your Journey Maps are not supposed to cover all edge cases, like your Lean Personas are not supposed to be accurate for all customers. Keep the map simple and workable.

The fourth step is to **identify the channels**. These channels may include anything from a retail store visit to an app download and from an advertisement in a magazine to a phone call with a support department. Any place, both physical and virtual, where your business has a presence is a possible channel to consider for your Journey Maps. For our business, our channels include our  website, blog, app, social media accounts, newsletter, Slack community, video chats, face-to-face meetings, surveys, speaking events, service desk, and more. For your business, I'm sure it will be different. Maybe your clients engage with you via Google Maps. Maybe you meet them on Tinder. I don't mind. It's not my business. It's yours.

As the fifth step, you **identify the touchpoints** that your customers have through each of the channels. Remember, your Journey Map is like a story. By stepping in your client's shoes and walking yourself through their journey, you should be able to find all major touchpoints. For example, "First they discover a blog post on Medium, then they read the white paper on our website, then they download the free trial version from the app  store, and so on." Not all channels are created equal and you may have to prioritize some over others. Because of the large number of available tools and technologies, there are many points of interaction nowadays. Complete coverage is impossible. Limit yourself to the typical paths.

As the sixth and final step, you **identify the experiences**. For each touchpoint, you may want to keep some notes. What are people's needs, emotions, and expectations at this point? What are the main tasks and the calls to action? What do the measurements say about what is really happening? Do customers experience a WOW moment or a WTF moment? Decorate your  Journey Map with the things you learn about people's journeys to make sure that you change your hypotheses into actual observations.

The Journey Map tool is one where several other practices come together. Besides choosing the Lean Personas and the areas of your Value Proposition Wheel, you should consider your customers' Jobs to Be Done and the current North Star Metric of your team. All of this together should result in ideas for Lean Experiments that can go onto your Product Backlog. All you do must be focused on delivering value to your customers, as early as you can.

Many organizations are blind to the experiences of their customers and users. They are unaware of the WOWs and the WTFs. But through tools such as customer interviews, user surveys, client observations, web analytics, help desk logs, product reviews, and social media listening, it is not that difficult to get a basic understanding of people's actual experiences with your product. Like the maps of the world, your Journey Maps start as best guesses and a bunch of hypotheses, but they can grow into accurate navigational tools that will help you locate the holy cows and fearful kittens across the entire experience.

For related notes, articles, books, examples, and downloads, check out this web page: https://startup-scaleup-screwup.com/journey-maps.

A Pirate's Tale

Find your way on the path to success, from awareness to revenue, measured with the Pirate Metrics.

"When will we get the iOS version?"

"After we have found Product/Market Fit."

"Oh, and when will you have Product/Market Fit?"

"Our Pirate Metrics should give us a signal."

"What are the Pirate Metrics?"

"I'm glad you asked."

The Pirate Metrics, also called the AARRR Metrics (or AAARRR Metrics), are a set of measurements proposed by Dave McClure, the founder of 500 Startups, that indicate how well your business model is working for you and your customers. Some people consider these metrics a great way to optimize a sales or marketing funnel. I consider them to be a good tool to improve many kinds of funnels. The Pirate Metrics are used by founders, entrepreneurs, and intrapreneurs to determine where their teams should be spending most of their time. (See Figure 23.1.)

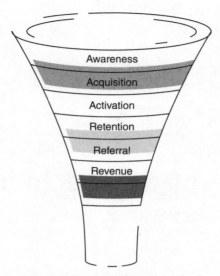

FIGURE 23.1   The Pirate Metrics (AAARRR)

You will notice that the various stages identified by the Pirate Metrics look similar to the stages of a high-level Journey Map. This is no coincidence. With a high-level Journey Map, you describe the experience of a customer from their first contact with your business to their enjoyment of your product. The Pirate Metrics describe a similar path, from a customer's awareness of your business to the new referrals they bring in. However, there are two important differences.

First, Journey Maps should always be described as experiences *from the client's viewpoint.* They tell the story of people's engagement with your business as seen through their eyes. The Pirate Metrics, however, describe stages that are relevant to *you*, not to your customer. They explain how successful *you* are at attracting, onboarding, and delighting new customers. It's similar, but not the same.

Second, Journey Maps can be created at various levels of detail, for any kind of customer experience. They can be cradle-to-grave, spanning many years, and they can cover a small interaction that happens on just one day. The Pirate Metrics, however, always cover the same stages of your business model: How well can you attract and keep customers?

Let's have a closer look, so you can see the differences for yourself.

The original Pirate Metrics tool consists of five stages that are easy to remember because of the mnemonic AARRR. However, entrepreneur and marketing expert Jordan Skole added an additional stage called **Awareness**, turning the tool into the AAARRR Metrics, with an extra A in front.

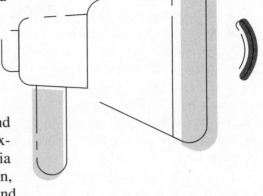

Skole suggested that any successful business transaction starts by introducing yourself to potential customers and getting them to take some action. For example, traditional advertising, social media advertising, search engine optimization, and affiliate programs are different tools and techniques to create awareness of your product in a market. In the awareness stage, the potential customer will come to know that your product exists. Without the creation of customer awareness, the other stages will achieve nothing. Your team might as well go bog snorkeling.

It is possible to have an Awareness stage on a high-level Journey Map. Customers who are going to love your product may want to become aware that it exists! In this first stage, it seems that the Pirate Metrics are aligned with the interests of your customers. Any happy business–customer relationship starts by first becoming aware of each other. Metrics that you can use to measure success in this stage are site visits, impressions, minutes of attention, page views, and so on.

When you are still validating your business model and seeking Business/Market Fit, you may not want to spend much time on the Awareness stage. You just need a small number of customers trying out your prototypes to know if your business works as intended. Only after you have found Business/Market Fit, when you have finished Stabilization (5) in the Business Lifecycle, it makes sense to open the gates and promote your product to a wider audience. This means that, for most businesses, Awareness is only relevant from Acceleration (6) and onward.

The second stage, **Acquisition**, is the first one that was covered by Dave McClure's original AARRR mnemonic. In other models, Acquisition is sometimes referred to as *conversion* or *interest*. This stage is about knowing who your potential customers are so that you can reach out to them in the future. It is about converting them from anonymous passersby to named and qualified prospects.

For example, you can get people to download a whitepaper in exchange for their e-mail address, ask them to follow you on Twitter, Facebook, or Instagram, get them to subscribe to your monthly newsletter, or offer them an ugly pen or stress ball in exchange for their business card at a trade show. Once you have obtained their data as a potential customer, you can gather other information about them that might be relevant. What you can measure in this stage are e-mail subscriptions, white paper downloads, webinar sign-ups, business cards, or anything else that is an indicator of people's interest in what you have to offer.

You should probably start working on the Acquisition stage before you focus on Awareness. This can make sense as soon as you have a Product Vision described. After all, when you have an idea about how you want to make people's lives better, you can start collecting information about those who want to be part of that adventure. I started doing this already in Initiation (1), long before our company was launched.

At this point, you can see how the purpose of the Pirate Metrics differs from that of your Journey Maps. In the Acquisition stage, your goal is to obtain information about potentially valuable customers. But, "Holy cow, giving you my contact details was such an amazing experience!" was said by no customer, ever. For your clients, a great experience could be getting an exclusive whitepaper, a useful newsletter, or free goodies at a conference. You can describe that with a Journey Map. The Journey Maps are about them; the Pirate Metrics are about you.

In the third stage, **Activation**, which is sometimes referred to as *consideration* or *interaction*, the client starts trying out your product. Here, your goal is to optimize the onboarding process so that people quickly and easily understand the value of your product. They need to see fast how it eases their Pains and brings them some Gains. It is the most important step in the funnel because the goal is for the customer to directly experience your value proposition. This means removing any superfluous steps that sit between a user trying your product and the time they experience their first WOW moment.

Some people define activation as the time it takes between the first trial of your product to the moment they don't want to part with it anymore. You could say it's the time between a first date and the acceptance of an engagement ring. From that moment on, you have a committed partner who is not just exploring the features and the options.

The metric you define here is going to be crucial for your product team and you will probably be able to use it as a North Star Metric. It is the one metric that expresses the actual value that users are getting from your product. Examples could be the order value per customer, the time spent in an app, or the number of megabytes or transactions per user on a SaaS platform. Given the importance of this stage, it seems obvious that this one should get all your focus during Validation (4). It is how you prove that your product works and that you have a happy customer.

In my Skype call with Peter Dowds, the CEO of Elder told me about some of the activation metrics that he uses with his teams.

> *An example metric for us would be we whether clients had an as-planned first week of care. So, for each customer, given the services and the processes we've designed, did the customer experience exactly that process in the first seven days, because we believe that has a high correlation with future retention. So, we have a zealous focus on that metric to make sure it is correct. Another one would be returning carers. Are carers returning to the customers? We believe continuity is crucial for retention, and we have a real focus on that. This being my second business, I'm a little more data-driven this time around than when I was a first-time founder. You really need to have those key KPIs and those North Stars—the metrics that matter.*
>
> *Peter Dowds, CEO and cofounder at Elder, London, United Kingdom*

The fourth stage is called **Retention**. It's not enough for people to be momentarily happy. For your business, and your relationship, it is important that your partner stays! You want people to come back on a regular basis or else you must spend all your time finding replacements. Acquiring new customers is a lot more expensive than keeping the existing ones. Retention, or *loyalty*, is an indicator of the amount of value that you generate for each other over time. If you can keep it high, you save a fortune on new engagement rings. Your goal is for your product to be sticky. If it's not, either the product is not good enough, or you are attracting the wrong people.

When your business has a subscription model, what you will be measuring is often churn (the percentage of people dropping out per month). When you have another type of revenue model, you could measure actual product usage, repeat purchases, or maintenance. Either way, when retention is low because too many customers drop your product, you have what we call a "leaky bucket." Fix the bucket first before pouring more water in. Focus on Retention before optimizing Awareness and Acquisition.

A popular retention metric was offered by Sean Ellis, the online marketer who coined the term *growth hacking*. The Sean Ellis Test suggests that you regularly survey a subset of your customers and ask them the question, "How would you feel if you could no longer use our product?" The possible answers are *Very disappointed*, *Somewhat disappointed*, *Not disappointed*, and *I don't use the product.* The idea is that, if at least 40 percent of your customers say they would be very disappointed, what you have is a *must-have* product. It is a signal that you could be very close to Product/Market Fit.

Retention is the perfect stage to focus on during Validation (4) and Stabilization (5). You will want to benchmark your retention against common metrics of other businesses in your specific industry, and you should focus on getting retention fixed before scaling up and creating more awareness.

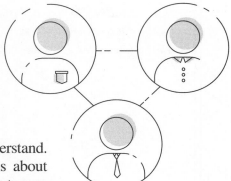

The fifth stage, **Referral**, is easy to understand. Sometimes called *advocacy* or *promotion*, it is about your customer's willingness to refer their friends to your product. Great performance on referrals is like achieving nirvana for scaleups because users who become advocates and bring in new customers are the best (and cheapest) salespeople to have. Enthusiastic users who are happy to promote your product and get pre-qualified referrals for you is the ultimate test of success of a working product.

What you can measure in this fifth stage are social shares, coupons, discount codes, and the number of referrals received. Some suggest that you can use a Net Promoter Score, but I feel very skeptical about this technique. Not a day goes by without some company asking me how likely I am to recommend their product to my friends. "On a scale of 0 to 10, how likely it is that you would recommend our selfie stick? Our bed bug spray? Our constipation relief tea?" I find it incredibly annoying and I never answer these surveys. Asking if someone would do something is quite different from them actually doing it. I suggest that you measure *actual* referrals rather than the *thought* of referrals. This is something to focus on from Stabilization (5) and onward, after you have collected evidence that your product works in Validation (4).

The final stage to discuss is **Revenue**, sometimes called *purchase*. This stage is the logical consequence of all the other ones. When you acquire enough users, activate most of them, get them to love your product, and help them to refer their friends, revenue should be a no-brainer.

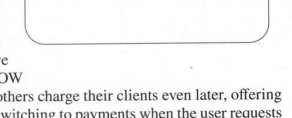

The revenue stage can sit at different points in your funnel. The best placement depends on the kind of revenue model that you have. Some businesses charge immediately at activation of a new customer. Others charge only after a certain amount of time ("get the first month free!"), to give new users a chance to experience a WOW moment in the Activation stage. Still others charge their clients even later, offering a freemium model first and then only switching to payments when the user requests additional features or upgrades.

The most relevant metrics here are Customer Lifetime Value (CLV or LTV) and Customer Acquisition Costs (CAC). CLV is how much revenue you earn, on average, over the lifetime of the customer relationship. CAC is the total amount you spend on sales and marketing to acquire that same customer. The ratio LTV:CAC is what you will want to optimize. You might already be charging customers from the Validation (4) stage, because feedback from paying users is always better than feedback from freemium users, but optimization of these revenue formulas is something you will probably only start doing from Stabilization (5) and onward.

The funnel as described by the Pirate Metrics looks similar to a high-level Journey Map. But Journey Maps are intended to describe a story from the user's or customer's perspective. Your client is not interested in referral or retention; *you* are. The Pirate Metrics describe what is important for you to make your business model a success. Don't make the mistake of thinking that customers want your business to be thriving. Most of them don't really care. They care more about looking good online and other personal problems. And you should care about their problems, as well.

The more your business model grows up, the more important the Pirate Metrics will become. In the beginning, your business is most helped with qualitative feedback from direct conversations with just a handful of early customers. It is only later that you will switch more and more to quantitative approaches with operational metrics. As long as you're still validating whether you have a working product, you can basically just focus on your Activation and Retention metrics. During Validation (4), that's where the heart of the problem is that needs to be solved.

For related notes, articles, books, examples, and downloads, check out this web page: https://startup-scaleup-screwup.com/pirate-metrics.

Test of the Twins

Learn about Growth Hacking and Conversion Rate Optimization with Split Tests, Multivariate Tests, and Cohort Analysis.

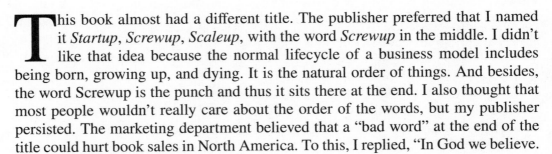

This book almost had a different title. The publisher preferred that I named it *Startup, Screwup, Scaleup*, with the word *Screwup* in the middle. I didn't like that idea because the normal lifecycle of a business model includes being born, growing up, and dying. It is the natural order of things. And besides, the word Screwup is the punch and thus it sits there at the end. I also thought that most people wouldn't really care about the order of the words, but my publisher persisted. The marketing department believed that a "bad word" at the end of the title could hurt book sales in North America. To this, I replied, "In God we believe. All others bring evidence."

To resolve the matter, I decided to do a test. I sent an e-mail over my mailing list of 10,000 people asking them how they liked my new book cover by clicking on it and rating it. What people didn't realize was that I sent out two versions of the cover. Half of the subscribers received a bright, pink cover with the title *Startup, Scaleup, Screwup*. The other half saw a bright, pink cover with *Startup, Screwup, Scaleup* in their mailbox. I had also split both groups into North America versus the Rest of the World. The result of this Split Test was fascinating.

The publisher and I were both correct. The book cover with the word *Screwup* in the middle did noticeably better in the click-through test, but only in North America. In the rest of the world, there was a slight preference for my version of the title, with *Screwup* at the end. But everyone complained equally about the color pink. I floated the idea of releasing the book under two titles in different regions, but this proved to be a logistical problem. So, I said, "Okay, then my title wins. We want to optimize sales globally and not just in North America. And we'll change the color from pink to white." It might have been the first argument that I won with real evidence rather than obstinance and persistence.

The Split Test that I described here counts as a Conversion Rate Optimization (CRO) technique. The purpose of a book cover (and its title) is to make people curious enough so that they read the book's description and the reviews. Using a simple test, I optimized the conversion of people from being aware of the book to being interested in the book. (Some titles do this better than others.) It is easy for us to disagree on book covers, landing page texts, newsletter designs, color palettes, and call-to-action buttons, and it is tempting to just use our intuition about what makes people convert from one stage to the next. CRO is the job of optimizing conversion across a funnel in a more data-driven way.

When I refer to funnels, the typical examples that come to mind are sales and marketing funnels with the standard stages that are covered by the Pirate Metrics. However, nothing prevents you from applying the same tools to other kinds of funnels, including those that address investors, donors, members, or even job candidates. You can also apply the same techniques to optimize the client experiences across Journey Maps. In this chapter, for the sake of brevity, I lump them all together by referring to them as funnels.

The more fashionable, younger sister of Conversion Rate Optimization is called *Growth Hacking*, a term that was coined by marketer Sean Ellis. It refers to the process of rapid experimentation to identify the simplest ways to improve the flow of customers through a sales or marketing funnel and thereby accelerate the growth of a business. Growth hackers operate in small, cross-functional teams consisting of marketers, developers, and product managers. You could say that Conversion Rate Optimization and Growth Hacking practically share the same purpose. However, CRO has traditionally focused mostly on content marketing in the Awareness and Acquisition stages, while the focus of Growth Hacking is more on product development and the entire funnel, including the Retention and Referral stages.

Growth hackers often say that they aim for the relentless growth of an existing business model. Personally, I don't like the word *growth* because I don't believe that growth should ever be a goal in itself. Growth for the sake of growth is the purpose of a cancer cell. But if your purpose is to make people happy with a great product then it is obvious that making *more* people happy requires you to grow your business. Why improve the lives of only 100 customers when you can change the lives of 100 million? *Impact stimulators* might have been a more accurate term than *growth hackers*, but I have never been a great talent at naming things.

The word *growth* should be a strong indication where in the Business Lifecycle you can best introduce Growth Hacking and Conversion Rate Optimization. Right! *After* you've validated your business model, in the Stabilization (5) and Acceleration (6) stages. The time to start hacking for growth is when your product actually works, and you can show great results for engagement and retention. It is a waste of your time to optimize and grow something that doesn't work. A growth hacking team can only accelerate a business model after Product/Market Fit, not before. Don't let your kid attach roller blades until after she can walk.

The book title test that I described earlier is what growth hackers and conversion rate optimizers call an A/B Test or Split Test. It is a simple test in which you divide your audience into two similar halves. You show them two different versions of the same thing and then measure which one has the best results. Like twins, they are almost the same, but not quite. The first, original version (A) is called the *control* and the new, alternative version (B) is called the *challenger*. In the example that I gave you, my original book title was the con-

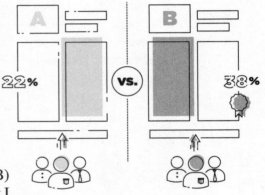

trol and the publisher's alternative suggestion was the challenger.

A/B Tests fit perfectly at the end of Lean Experiments. Does an experiment make things better or worse? Let's validate with an A/B Test! In fact, Split Tests are a common tool in many other hypothesis-driven contexts, including product development and service design, where there is a need for the validation of assumptions. It is probably unrealistic to split-test every new feature with quantitative measurements, so the recommendation is to do this only when the effects of a good or bad choice can be significant, and when early, qualitative signals don't show a clear winner among the options.

For a proper A/B Test, what you show the two parts of your audience, and how you treat them, must be the same except for the variable that you are testing, or else you can't be certain about the results. For example, in the book title test, I did not send the test for version A in the morning and the one for version B in the evening, because the time difference might have polluted the measurements.

Melanie Wessels, an Agile Coach at Booking.com, shared with me how much her employer values testing.

> *We A/B test every single thing. We do it in small steps, resulting in rapid innovation. For example, the way people use street addresses in China is not the same as we use them in the Western world. And, of course, we're trying to grow in China, but it's really hard because there are competitors out there who are really big. We just want to make sure that our Chinese customers feel that our site feels familiar. That the experience feels comfortable for them. So there was this experiment we did with street addresses and, in just a short time, we were able to turn things around and create street addresses that made way more sense to Chinese customers. It's these kinds of simple things. Maybe this is a stupid example. But everything is tested. Everything.*
>
> *Melanie Wessels, Agile Coach at Booking.com, Amsterdam,*
> *The Netherlands*

After the interview, Melanie and I went for a walk outside, in Amsterdam city center, to personally test a really nice coffee.

Sometimes, the things you want to test don't easily sort themselves into two buckets called version A and B. The more complicated alternative to the A/B Test is called the Multivariate Test. With this type of test, there is more than one variable and possibly more than one version per variable. For example, a multivariate test of a landing page on a website could include multiple color palettes, various font sizes, and a number of positions of the call-to-action button.

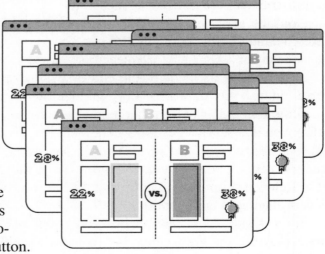

Figuring out the optimal combination of values for multiple variables and versions requires doing a tremendous number of tests.

Fortunately, there are software solutions available to do all the heavy lifting for you. An important requirement, however, is that you have an audience that is large enough to run the tests. The more variables and versions you have, the bigger the test audience needs to be, and the longer it takes to achieve meaningful outcomes. I'd say you can safely postpone the usage of this technique to the Acceleration (6) and Crystallization (7) stages. In earlier stages, you probably don't have an audience of the required size.

When I tested the book title, I performed an additional test with an online tool that offered me simple demographics. It turned out that, on average, older people preferred the publisher's alternative book title (with *Screwup* in the middle) while younger people preferred my version (with *Screwup* at the end). This makes sense because the more my age scales up, the more I realize that screwing up, down, and sideways, was something I did more often when I was younger.

Publishers don't normally sell the same books to different age groups under different titles, but differentiating a product for age ranges, genders, regions, or industries can be easy when it is an app, website, or other digital product. You can optimize your funnel by considering different customer segments. For segment X, variant A of your product could be preferable, while for segment Y, it could be variant B. You modify your product and your communication in such a way that it shows different variants depending on which customers you're dealing with. Offer emojis, stickers, and cyber-slang to the young ones. Write fully qualified and punctuated sentences for people like me.

Don't be surprised to find out that everything is interrelated. For example, a tweak to a button that increases the response rate for native English speakers in North America could hurt the engagement among non-native English speakers in Europe. If you don't identify the segments, you might not be aware of any change at all because, in the aggregate, the response rate could stay the same. You'll never know until you measure.

You can take Conversion Rate Optimization one step further by doing Cohort Analysis. A cohort is a group of people that you follow to study their behaviors over time. With a Split Test, you focus on just one action. With Cohort Analysis, you focus on a sequence of actions. You cluster people together who share a value for one specific variable. And then you analyze how the flow of engagement across your product is different for one cohort compared to another.

For example, you can find out where people came from who arrived on your blog or website. You can define cohorts such as Google Search, Facebook Ads, Twitter updates, and Direct links, and then analyze how the behaviors of those cohorts differ by using Google Analytics. Another example could be your weekly newsletter, where different cohorts can be defined as the groups of people who acted on any specific newsletter campaign and then you follow what they're doing after responding to your e-mail.

We call them segment-based cohorts when you cluster a group of customers from the same segment and then follow their behaviors over time to understand how their actions differ from other segments. For example, you might discover that customers who found your product through Google Search have a higher retention rate than those who found you through Facebook ads. Or you might discover that customers who used a discount coupon have much higher churn than those who signed up without a promotional offer. Such information is super-valuable because it can help you optimize your marketing strategy. A sales or marketing funnel is a great tool to have, but it becomes even more powerful with Cohort Analysis.

A special kind of cohort is the time-based cohort, which is about grouping people together based on the time slots in which they found, accessed, or purchased your product, or performed some other action for the first time. When growth hackers use time-based cohorts, they often cluster customers by weeks or months and then analyze the various stages of the funnel separately for each. With this technique, they can discover things such as an increase in activation for customers who joined since week 12, or a decrease in retention for users who arrived after the summer. Using time-based cohort analysis, you can retrospectively correlate changes in the metrics with product changes and new features that happened around certain dates. It is a technique that will be very powerful from the moment you have found Product/Market Fit and are getting ready to scale things up.

A/B Testing, Multivariate Testing, and Cohort Analysis are important practices in the toolbox of growth hackers and conversion rate optimizers. They typically fit in the Sensitize stream of the Innovation Vortex because these tools are all about creating awareness of the progress that a team is making.

It makes you wonder why some refer to this field as growth *hacking*. Testing and discovering the best messages in your communication, the most effective features in your product, and the proper segmentation of your audience, is not just hacking. It is the disciplined and professional optimization of your sales or marketing funnel. But it comes with a danger, as well. All too often, people have a tendency of diving into the details of tweaking features, texts, colors, and font sizes to increase conversion percentages so that they achieve rapid near-term growth. But in doing so, they lose sight of the bigger picture.

With the large amounts of data that businesses have at their disposal, it is easy to get lost in numbers and to focus only on what is immediately measurable and optimizable. But a climb to the top is rarely a line that only goes up. In fact, if you insist on making every individual change an improvement, you might never even reach that top. Sometimes, it takes one step down to make two steps up. Don't confuse the optimization of many small, trivial steps with optimization of the entire journey. Stay focused on your Product Vision, Value Proposition Wheel, North Star Metric, and the Journey Maps you created for your clients.

Sebastien Phlix and Miloš Lalić, the product guys I talked with at Typeform in Barcelona, agreed with me.

> *What we're trying to nail now is being detailed about the right things—prioritizing what are the main interaction points and really, really taking care of them. And for the other things, just deliberately de-prioritizing them. That's what product management does. But we really want to take it to the next level. That means customers interviews, lots of iterations, A/B testing—all of that stuff to make sure we're really nailing this.*
> *Sebastien Phlix, senior product manager, and Miloš Lalić, director of product at Typeform, Barcelona, Spain*

And I think they nailed it well, because I'm a heavy user of Typeform myself.

My own team is trying to do the right thing, as well. When you're still searching for Product/Market Fit, like us, doing the right thing beats doing things right. Exploration is about finding the right thing to focus on as a business. Execution is about doing things right from an operational perspective. Exploration comes before execution. First do the right thing, and then do that thing right.

It is far too early for my team to do any Multivariate Testing or Cohort Analysis. But we could start training our growth hacking muscles by doing some simple Split Tests. Right now, my team is creating a new Journey Map for crowd investors who want to take part in our upcoming Agile Funding rounds. We could soon be working on optimization of our new Equity Crowdfunding funnel. That's going to be very interesting.

For related notes, articles, books, examples, and downloads, check out this web page: https://startup-scaleup-screwup.com/split-tests.

Culture Clash

Identify Core Values, create a Culture Code, and use stories and rewards to prepare your business for scaling.

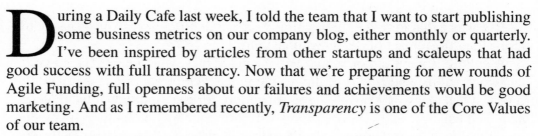

During a Daily Cafe last week, I told the team that I want to start publishing some business metrics on our company blog, either monthly or quarterly. I've been inspired by articles from other startups and scaleups that had good success with full transparency. Now that we're preparing for new rounds of Agile Funding, full openness about our failures and achievements would be good marketing. And as I remembered recently, *Transparency* is one of the Core Values of our team.

Some time ago, I was trying to recall what the other Core Values are that our team agreed upon during a team offsite in Copenhagen. But for at least an hour, I failed to remember the outcome of our discussions. However, suddenly, I had an idea. I opened Slack and I typed the word "mnemonic" in the search box. Sure enough, there it was! A message from me that I sent to the team, three months earlier:

"I found a mnemonic for our top five values: PETIT: Passion, Empathy, Trust, Integrity, and Transparency. Maybe now we will be able to remember them more easily."

Well, that little trick certainly helped a lot.

As a startup or scaleup founder, entrepreneur, or intrapreneur, you have many number one jobs. Sometimes, your number one job is hiring a great team.

Other times, your number one job is acquiring funds or customers. At many points in between, your number one job is not to screw things up. But a significant portion of your time, your number one job is developing the right culture for your business.

Daniel Krauss, cofounder and CIO of Flixbus, agreed with me.

> *Building up and maintaining a proper culture and scaling the organization with good talent, transparently and fair, deciding who can join, who must leave, who to promote, etcetera—is the most challenging part of my job. It's much more challenging than I originally thought it would be. All the other challenges, like scaling our platform, there are solutions for that. And if you managed the organizational part, then you have people who will tackle many of those challenges with the available solutions. But yeah, this is still the most challenging part of my work.*
>
> *Daniel Krauss, cofounder and CIO of Flixbus, Berlin, Germany*

Ever since that interview, every time I see a green-orange Flixbus passing by, I think about the impact of organizational culture.

A culture is a system of shared beliefs and values, which gives rise to certain behaviors, habits, and rituals of the people in it. Every organization has a culture. In fact, it has many. It probably has a subculture for each individual team, department, and business unit. These cultures will form, one way or another. If you don't intentionally grow a culture yourself, you will get one that you probably don't want. So, it's best to make culture growth a number one priority. Especially when it looks like your business will be scaling up soon.

A good culture is a fundamental requirement for scaling your business in a healthy way. The larger the organization gets, the more decisions people make without your involvement. When you are not around to make or discuss these decisions, the best way to influence them is through a shared vision and a shared culture. In other words, an organizational culture is what you put in place to influence behaviors in the company because you can't scale yourself.

By accepting that culture is the set of beliefs and values that influence people's behaviors, you can rule out some things that are *not* part of the culture. Culture is not motivational posters, T-shirts, hoodies, team lunches, foosball tables, free massages, and Friday afternoon drinks. Such things can be the *result* of your culture, but they don't *define* your culture. Instead, culture is the character of the organization as exemplified by how people behave toward each other and toward the organization's stakeholders. Your culture is not your values listed in an employee handbook. Your culture is the *act* of communicating important things in an employee handbook.

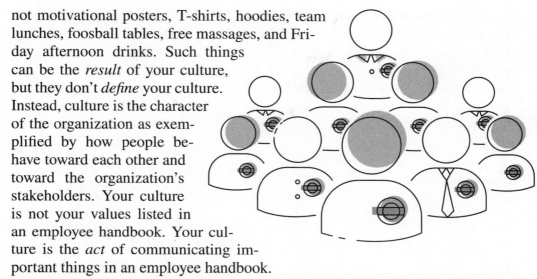

What are good values for startups and scaleups? When do we consider a shared belief so important that we elevate it to a *Core* Value? Well, this is an easy thing to check. A shared belief is a Core Value when you are willing to fire someone for consistently not behaving according to that value. A shared belief is a Core Value when you decide not to hire one of the greatest talents in the world because he or she does not express a willingness to honor that value. A shared belief is a Core Value when you are willing to give up money just so you can stick to what you think is right. Core Values have the power to be painful.

For example, equality is a Core Value when founders are ready to fire people for acts of discrimination, racism, sexism, or bigotry. Integrity is a Core Value when business leaders refuse to bribe someone to get ahead of a competitor in the market. If you want to know what the true values of a company are, look at the decisions that managers make when there is a lot of money at stake. Observe the things that the leaders choose *not* to do that might hurt them in their wallets. Core Values should be difficult for many people to uphold. When everyone easily agrees and acts according to some values, then it is no use to even mention them. Pick only Core Values that, to some extent, repel the wrong people and makes decisions painful for everyone else.

Sergei Anikin, CTO at Pipedrive, had an interesting example to share with me.

We have feature requests coming from our customers that are going against our values. We can honestly tell our customers that these features are never going to end up on the platform. A very simple example is people—especially managers—are constantly asking us to implement some mandatory fields where the system would require users to enter specific data. This goes against our principle that our tool should never prevent salespeople from actually selling. We understand the importance of complete data, but that shouldn't stand in the way of a person being able to sell in a flow. They don't want to see, "No, you cannot sell now until you fill in these 10 required fields," when they don't have that information. They just want to move forward. And then the managers say, "Yeah, but we need this data." And we say, "Sorry, but your salespeople cannot sell if they need all the data crunched first."

Sergei Anikin, CTO at Pipedrive, Tallinn, Estonia

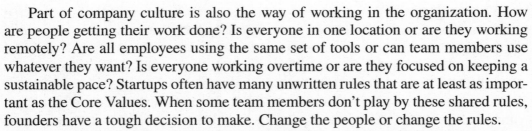

Part of company culture is also the way of working in the organization. How are people getting their work done? Is everyone in one location or are they working remotely? Are all employees using the same set of tools or can team members use whatever they want? Is everyone working overtime or are they focused on keeping a sustainable pace? Startups often have many unwritten rules that are at least as important as the Core Values. When some team members don't play by these shared rules, founders have a tough decision to make. Change the people or change the rules.

As an example of startup culture, Matt Ellsworth from 500 Startups shared with me how startups around the world have different values regarding working hours.

When I first started working with European startups—and this doesn't apply to all European countries or all startups, for sure—but in general, I was like, "Oh, man. Don't you feel the urgency?" It seemed to me they weren't stressed out enough, which was a really weird feeling. I think it's hard, in general, for people to find the equanimity between working hard enough and not overworking. But that was a big difference that I noticed between European startups and U.S.-based startups.

I think, actually, depending on what stage your company is in, you could probably land somewhere in the middle, and that would be perfect. Maybe that's just the American in me. I don't know. But I don't see a problem with the startup scene in general, the glorification of the overworking, the insane hours. There's a difference between being inspired by your own work, working a bunch of hours because you want to when you're in the early stages, and being able to maintain a company for 5 to 10 years, which you won't be able to do if all you're doing is sprinting all the time. There are going to be periods of intense work where it's like, "Okay, for the next month, we have to get something out the door. But after that, we should have a planned period of time where we're relaxing our work schedule. We are not getting burnt out."

Matt Ellsworth, partner at 500 Startups, Paris, France

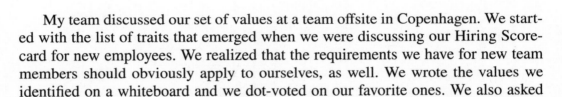

My team discussed our set of values at a team offsite in Copenhagen. We started with the list of traits that emerged when we were discussing our Hiring Scorecard for new employees. We realized that the requirements we have for new team members should obviously apply to ourselves, as well. We wrote the values we identified on a whiteboard and we dot-voted on our favorite ones. We also asked two missing team members to vote on those values remotely. What emerged was the set Passion, Empathy, Trust, Integrity, and Transparency, with the nice mnemonic PETIT, the one that I spontaneously remembered.

I consider them all Core Values because I can certainly imagine not hiring a great candidate when they lack a passion for helping organizations change more easily, which is our company's purpose. I can imagine firing someone for repeatedly violating the trust among team members. I can also imagine not signing with a new customer when they require us to operate in secrecy rather than with transparency. So yes, I believe we found a good set of Core Values. Living up to them might be painful at times. There needs to be some clashing.

I believe that the character of a business evolves in a way similar to the character of a person. In the early years, the personality of a child is still quite changeable and, as a parent, you have some chance at steering it in a certain direction. But over time, when the kid grows up, the mindset will settle, and no amount of steering will have any desired effect, as the parent of probably every teenager can confirm.

For startups and scaleups, the process might be similar. In the beginning, the default culture of a startup is defined by whatever the founders considered important. But when the first additional team members arrive, the character of the business changes and culture is in a state of flux. However, as long as there is a small team, there is still a tight circle of relationships, making it easy to define new rules for future collaboration.

Over time, however, when the business grows larger, it gets progressively more difficult to maintain the close relationships that the original team once had. It then comes down to the first team members to teach the existing culture to newer employees. Hopefully, they will have great stories to share and some Core Values to hire against. The original founders will have less of an immediate impact, but their influence will be indirect, by having prepared the organization and the earliest team members for that larger scale. Once the business has become a teenager, and is scaling up rapidly, the existing culture will be tremendously difficult to change.

Many businesses take the effort of codifying their values using culture books, posters, and coffee mugs. If that's what you want, go ahead. I'm sure reminding people every now and then what the agreed-upon Core Values are can't really hurt. And it might be nice to have a mnemonic that helps you remember them. But please, when you design a Culture Code slide deck, don't turn this document into a promotional thing. There are too many Culture Codes online that look like marketing blah blah, full of inauthentic photos and insincere quotes. Don't be one of those fake companies. Keep it real. If you want a culture book, ask your team to help you make one. Leaders should not define a set of values without any involvement of everyone else.

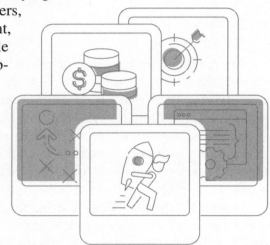

And don't believe for a moment that slide decks and posters are going to have any measurable impact on people. We influence each other through stories and recognition, not mnemonics. Team members remember the value stories they tell each other. They will also remember the behaviors that were rewarded, and the ones that were punished. They won't easily remember the Core Values they once wrote on a whiteboard.

Jenni Tolonen, CEO of Management Events, gave me an example of how values come alive at her company.

When I go to our Kuala Lumpur office, every time, we start the staff meeting with the values. This started by accident because the first time I did the staff meeting, we discussed our values. The second time I asked them, "Okay, do we remember the company values by heart?" And then I asked, "Why do we have these values? And do they resonate in your daily life?" And the third time I went there, I didn't ask about the values. This was unintentional, but then one of my sales directors came to me after the meeting and said, "The staff was wondering why you didn't go through the values because they had been making notes of how to answer your questions."

Now we discuss those values every time. And I always ask, "Why do we have a value, such as passion for customers?" And then they're like, "If customers like our products and they come back, that's good for our business. They pay our salaries." So, we try to get to the root cause. The point is not that they can just repeat the values. And I've asked examples, like, "How has passion for customers come alive this week?" And an answer could be like, "Today a customer called, and we had an invoice missing, and I worked with finance and I solved that problem for them." So, we reinforce the behaviors that are based on our values.

Jenni Tolonen, CEO of Management Events, Helsinki, Finland

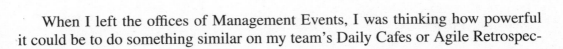

When I left the offices of Management Events, I was thinking how powerful it could be to do something similar on my team's Daily Cafes or Agile Retrospectives.

As a founder, entrepreneur, or intrapreneur, you want to grow a healthy culture in your business to prepare it for scaling up. To achieve this, your focus should be on stories and rewards. Highlight and celebrate the behaviors that have been exemplary among your team. When a person or a team has done something that resonates with one of the Core Values, make sure to let everyone in the company know. You have to make these values explicit, not by printing them on coffee mugs, but by recognizing publicly those who have made tough decisions and overcame great challenges. The culture of your company is defined by who you hire, how you reward and recognize people, and how you let some of them go. But most of all, they are defined by how you lead by example.

I write books and blog posts to express my *Passion* for organizational change. I am awful at practicing *Empathy* so whenever I ask a team member an honest question about their health or family, I feel proud of myself for having done what's important. I compensate my struggle with empathy with a generous amount of

Trust in the team with all the responsibilities I have delegated to them. I hope that nobody doubts my *Integrity* because I always try to be fair and honest in my dealings with employees and other stakeholders. And now that you've come to the end of this book, there is probably nothing more I need to add about the topic of *Transparency*. I am practically an open book. Like the one in your hands.

The mnemonic spells PETIT. It means small. It's a fine word for a business such as ours.

Maybe in a few years, we have a new set of values that spells the word GRAND.

Or maybe they will spell ZERO.

We'll see.

For related notes, articles, books, examples, and downloads, check out this web page: https://startup-scaleup-screwup.com/culture-code.

Epilogue

The whiteboard was nearly full when Sasa Stamenkovic, chief lean and agile coach, finished drawing how iZettle in Stockholm had reorganized themselves into a new organizational structure.

> *We are trying to work with … call it values streams or domains (or whatever you want to call them). They take a product to market, which includes discovery, product development, marketing, sales, the whole business. We try to make those as streamlined as possible throughout the whole business. So it's not like product design has their flow, and then it goes to marketing, and then sales. No, it's more like a cross-functional go-to-market team that takes care of everything, including the feedback that goes back to development. Does that make sense?*
> *Sasa Stamenkovic, chief lean and agile coach at iZettle,*
> *Stockholm, Sweden*

Yes, that makes total sense to me. Call them business models, value streams, domains, or value units. I don't care much about the specific terminology. We mean the same thing. Our point of focus in business is the value-creating entity, which we can describe as a business model or a value stream, plus everyone who is involved in creating and maintaining it.

This value unit has a typical growth path that I describe with the Shiftup Business Lifecycle. It starts up, it scales up, and at some point, it screws up. I explain how to make that value unit work with the Shiftup Business Quilt, which reveals that a successful business is stitched together from many business model pieces. Throughout its lifecycle, each value unit first mainly explores and then primarily executes its business model. We can describe the innovative aspects of that growth process with the seven streams of the Shiftup Innovation Vortex. Finally, if you organize things well as a large organization, your company is a whole family full of such value units. Each one follows its own path along the business lifecycle.

Et voilà, that was the summary of this book.

There are only six hours to go until I must send this manuscript to the publisher. My team is preparing the launch of tomorrow's crowdfunding. I trust them to get this done without me. My mailbox shows me some final artwork from the illustrator that I can add to a few chapters at the last minute. The heater next to me is keeping me warm here in my little home office in Brussels. And there's another laundry in the washing machine. That horrible thing is insatiable.

Meanwhile, I'm already thinking of the next project.

Tuomas Syrjänen, cofounder at Futurice in Helsinki, Finland, and his colleague Eeva Raita, head of culture advisory, told me about the layered approach their company uses to optimize its innovative capabilities, while the employees near us were enjoying themselves around the company's espresso machine.

> *It's like an onion. We have something that we own 100 percent and some things of which we are the majority owner. And then there are cases where we own just 15 or 20 percent. And there are businesses where we just invested some money without any management involvement at all. We have been able to balance on this edge between order and chaos, where there's a huge amount of energy, innovation, and so on. But there's still enough alignment to make sure that the company goes in the desired direction.*
> *Tuomas Syrjänen, cofounder at Futurice,*
> *Helsinki, Finland*

Traditional corporations usually have a terrible way of organizing their innovative efforts. R&D departments, innovation committees, innovation pipelines—I've seen it all. Nothing ever works.

The smartest way to innovate as a company is to leave old structures and frameworks behind. Reorganize yourself as a family of businesses. Treat all family members differently, depending on where they are in their business lifecycle. Turn the entire company into one large innovation funnel, full of startups, scaleups, and yes, also a decent number of screwups. Every family has them.

I could write an entire second book about shaking up old organizations, speeding up their innovative efforts, and funding value units that are shifting up their lifecycles. Shakeup, Speedup, and Shiftup. Hmmm. My remaining interview and research materials would get me a long way.

Innovation requires letting go of the old ways of doing things and embracing the new. Out of all my interviews with startups and scaleups across Europe, the very first one was with my friend Marcin Floryan, director of engineering at Spotify, in Stockholm, Sweden. It was freezing that day. I warmed myself on a cafe latte while I tried to find the building.

> *As you know, at Spotify, we like to call everything by our own special names, such as tribes, squads, and guilds. There are good reasons for doing this. We tried to pick terms that weren't already established in the industry so that we can break away from the norms and the ways of thinking that existed elsewhere.*
>
> *Marcin Floryan, director of engineering, Spotify,*
> *in Stockholm, Sweden*

Marcin told me much more that day, which I will share with you another time. Maybe in that next book I'm thinking about.

After the interview, on my way out, I stole a copy of the colorful little booklet that tells the entire story of Spotify. Maybe, one day, I can make one of these about my company. There's still a lot to do.

Acknowledgments

No book is written alone, yadda, yadda, yadda. So, here we go.

A big thanks to my colleagues at Agility Scales, both former and current team members: Ceyda Erten, Dejan Nesic, Dariusz Baciński, Harald Paul, Iain Thackrah, Kirill Zotin, Mathias Daus, Paula Cassin, Paweł Urban, Pedro Medas, Ruaridh Currie, Thomas Kuryura, and Tolga Özdemir. You all inspired me to try crazy things and you went along with it and followed my lead. Thanks for your trust in me!

A few dozen CEOs, CTOs, CIOs, agile coaches, team leaders, and other employees from startups and scaleups all over Europe have graciously made themselves available for interviews. I learned a ton from them and I was only able to include small fragments of those interviews in this book. Nevertheless, a big thanks to each one for sharing their insights, successes, and failures.

You will thank *me* for not naming all beta reviewers individually because this might have increased the price of the book. There were 129 of them! Each reviewed between one to three chapters per person and this book would not have been as good as it is now without the many corrections and suggestions I received. Thanks to each and every one.

I also thank my book team: Brandon Brown (logistics), Juan Franco (design), and Sara Pedraz (marketing). You're doing a great job helping me turn this idea that I had about startups and scaleups into a global success and a lot of new business. Fingers crossed.

Last, but certainly not least: Thanks and hugs to my dear Raoul. Where would I be without you? Probably in some penthouse in London, reading a science fiction novel, on my own. And where's the fun in that?

About the Author

With his company Agility Scales, Jurgen is inventing the future of organizational agility. Why are we wasting our time learning how to manage companies, when very soon computers will navigate us through our work lives and help us to lead and manage our teams?

As a serial founder, successful entrepreneur, author, and speaker, Jurgen is pioneering management to help creative organizations survive and thrive in the twenty-first century. He offers concrete games, tools, and practices, so you can introduce better management, with fewer managers. He also offers a platform for you to share your practices and stories with the rest of the world.

Jurgen calls himself a *creative networker*. But sometimes he's a writer, speaker, trainer, entrepreneur, illustrator, manager, blogger, reader, dreamer, leader, freethinker, or … Dutch guy. Inc.com has called him a Top 50 Leadership Expert and a Top 100 Leadership Speaker. Since 2008, Jurgen writes a popular blog at NOOP.NL, offering ideas on the creative economy, agile management, organizational change, and personal development. He is the author of the book *Management 3.0*, which describes the role of the manager in agile organizations. And he wrote the little book *How to Change the World*, which describes a supermodel for change management. His last book (before the one you have in your hands) was *Managing for Happiness*, which offers practical ideas for engaging workers, improving work, and delighting clients.

Index